THE LITTLE
BLACK BOOK OF

NEW YORK

The Essential Guide to the

Quintessential City

D1115085

MAPS BY DAVID LINDROTH, INC.

ILLUSTRATED BY
KERREN BARBAS STECKLER

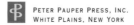

PETER PAUPER PRESS, INC.
WHITE PLAINS, NEW YORK

FOR NINA AND JACK,
TRUE NEW YORKERS

*The editors would like to extend a special
thanks to cartographer David Lindroth
for his tireless efforts on this project.*

Proofreader: JCommunications, LLC

Designed by Heather Zschock

Illustrations copyright © 2006 Kerren Barbas Steckler

The Map is copyrighted by the MTA. Used by permission.
Neighborhood maps © 2011 David Lindroth Inc.

The publisher has made every effort to ensure that the content of this book was current at time of publication. It's always best, however, to confirm information before making final travel plans, since telephone numbers, Web sites, prices, hours of operation, and other facts are always subject to change. The publisher cannot accept responsibility for any consequences arising from the use of this book. We value your feedback and suggestions. Please write to: Editors, Peter Pauper Press, Inc., 202 Mamaroneck Avenue, Suite 400, White Plains, New York 10601-5376.

Visit us at www.peterpauper.com

THE LITTLE
BLACK BOOK OF
NEW YORK

CONTENTS

INTRODUCTION

New York City is immense, the biggest city in the United States and one of the biggest in the world, with a population of over 8 million covering 305 square miles. It's packed with some of the most famous restaurants, museums, buildings, and visitor sites in the world. Our pocket-sized *Little Black Book of New York* covers the top picks for each neighborhood, in an easy-to-use and un-intimidating format for those new to the city. You can take this book with you anywhere in Manhattan—knowing it will provide a succinct list of what's essential in every neighborhood, from art galleries to architecture—and because of its size, most people won't even know you're a tourist!

We've broken Manhattan down by neighborhoods, and then grouped adjoining neighborhoods into eight individual maps and chapters for convenience; and there's also a public transportation map at the back. If you'd rather look things up by their specific names, we've included an index, too. We hope you enjoy your visit, and that you'll find all you need in this Little Black Book to navigate this great city with pleasure and aplomb.

NEW YORK STREET GRID

New York is a pretty easy city to get around, thanks to its grid plan that was adopted in 1811. The plan called for 12 numbered avenues running north and south roughly parallel to the Hudson River, and about 155 cross streets running east and west. Exceptions to this plan include Broadway, which was in place at the time of the 1811 plan. It cuts an angle from southeast to northwest. Rather than change it, this was turned to the city's advantage by creating "squares" wherever Broadway crossed a north-south avenue. The famed Broadway is now practically synonymous with New York City. Greenwich Village (below 14th Street) was also able to keep its confusing street pattern (largely because it had been kept separate from the rest of the city by a yellow fever and cholera epidemic in the early 1800s). The streets of the Village are for the most part the same as they were in the early 1800s, with crooked paths best suited for walking. The winding roads can make this area a bit challenging to navigate, but the charming cobblestone streets are well worth it.

HOW TO USE THIS GUIDE

We have included eight fold-out maps, by neighborhood sections, with color-coded keys to help you find the places listed in the text. **Red** symbols indicate **Places to See**, which include landmarks, arts & entertainment, and fun stuff to do with kids. **Blue** symbols indicate **Places to Eat & Drink**, which include restaurants, bars, and nightlife. **Orange** symbols indicate **Where to Shop**. And **Green** symbols indicate **Where to Stay**.

Here are our keys for restaurant and hotel costs:

Restaurants
Cost of an appetizer and main course without drinks

($)	Up to $25
($$)	$25-$45
($$$)	$45-$70
($$$$)	$70 and up

Hotels
Cost per night

($)	$50-$125
($$)	$125-$250
($$$)	$250-$400
($$$$)	$400 and up

PUBLIC TRANSPORTATION

The public transportation map at the back lets you know how to get around fast and easily on the subways. We've started each neighborhood section with a listing of which subways (and subway stops) to use to get to the neighborhood.

A free copy of the subway map is available at any subway station booth. The main way to pay for public transportation is the MetroCard®, a magnetic fare card, which is sold at all subway station booths, and through vending machines (that accept cash, debit, and credit cards) that are in many subway stations and at many other locations. You can use a MetroCard at all subway stations and on all public and many private buses within New York City. If you use a MetroCard, you can transfer free of charge between subway and bus, bus and subway, bus and bus. One-Day Fun Pass and seven- to 30-day unlimited ride MetroCards are also available.

SUBWAY TIPS

Listen Up

As with any mass public transportation system, there are bound to be service changes, repairs, interruptions, etc. Don't panic! Just listen to the conductors for their specific directions, read the signs posted, and don't be afraid to ask other passengers questions. New Yorkers (contrary to their bad rap) are helpful and love to dispense directions to show off their New York knowledge.

Downtown-Uptown

When you're entering a subway station, pay attention to whether you're using the "Downtown" entrance or the "Uptown" entrance. They're usually right across the street from each other. You don't want to end up paying twice because you went through the wrong entrance! Some of the bigger stations don't split their entrances on the street level (for example, Times Square). In those cases, you can choose the uptown or downtown side once you get underground.

SEASONAL EVENTS

In spring, flowers bloom and New Yorkers come out of hibernation. Summer is balmy and bawdy, and with many residents retreating to the country or the shore, it's easier to get a table at that exclusive restaurant or to grab an otherwise tough ticket on Broadway. Fall offers some of the most beautiful weather of the year, and the occasional chill foretells the arrival of winter, when sparkling snow and city lights combine to create a true wonderland. No matter what season, the Greatest City in the World offers world class entertainment, sports, and special events.

Spring:

St. Patrick's Day Parade (March 17th)—Just days before the official start of spring, New York's finest come out in droves for the annual parade. Fifth Avenue becomes a sea of police officers, firefighters, and plenty of leprechauns to celebrate the green holiday *(Fifth Ave, 44th to 86th Sts., www.saintpatricksdayparade.com, starts at 11AM).*

Easter Parade (Easter Sunday)—No longer limited to the elite, the parade that inspired the song marches up Fifth Avenue between 49th and 57th, starting at 10AM. You can put on your own Easter bonnet—with all the frills upon it—and join in. Or just sit back and watch the spectacle.

Play Ball! (Early April)—New York claims to be the birthplace of America's pastime, and while there is some dispute about that, Opening Day for the fabled **New York Yankees** *(www.yankees.com, 718-293-4300)* or **New York Mets** *(www.mets.com, 718-507-TIXX)* is a sure sign of spring. For a more intimate experience, cheer on one of New York's minor league teams. The **Brooklyn Cyclones**, Class A affiliate of the Mets, play at KeySpan Park on New York's famous Coney Island *(www.brooklyncyclones.com, 718-449-8497)*. Or catch a great game along with unparalleled views of the Manhattan skyline watching the Staten Island Yankees *(www.siyanks.com, 718-720-9265)*. The Yankees Class A farm team plays at Richmond County Bank Ballpark at St. George, which is located just steps away from the **Staten Island Ferry**, one of the best bargains in town.

Summer:

Street Fairs (Every weekend from late spring to early fall on various streets)—Throughout summer, New Yorkers reclaim some city streets from taxis, buses, and bike messengers. New York's street fairs offer unique merchandise, great ethnic food, and some even have live entertainment *(www.nycstreetfairs.com)*.

Shakespeare in the Park (June–August)—New York's cultural icons enjoy a little fresh air, too. See stars like Meryl Streep and Philip Seymour Hoffman and many more perform Shakespeare's plays at the Delacorte Theater in Central Park. Tickets are free (limit 2 per person), but they go fast *(212-260-2400, www. publictheater.org for schedule)*.

New York Philharmonic (July)—The nation's oldest symphony orchestra performs outdoor concerts in all five boroughs during the summer *(www.nyphil.org)*.

Summer Friday Music Concerts (June–August)—Catch the stars out in the daytime! The network morning shows are in a battle for ratings and for the best concert acts, which you can catch for free outside on summer Fridays. ABC's *Good Morning America* broadcasts their concerts from Central Park *(www.abcnews. go.com/GMA)*, and NBC's *Today Show* broadcasts in Rockefeller Plaza *(49th Street between 5th and 6th Aves., www.todayshow.com)*.

Autumn:

Broadway on Broadway (Mid-September)—The new season on Broadway starts in September, and the League of American Theaters kicks it off every year with a free outdoor concert in Times Square with highlights of the new offerings *(details in August at www.broadwayonbroadway.com)*. Like what you see? Reduced price theater tickets are available the day of the performance at the Theater Development Fund's "TKTS" booths, located in Times Square and at the South Street Seaport *(www.tdf.org, credit cards, cash, and travelers checks accepted)*.

Village Halloween Parade (October 31st, evening)—In New York's Bohemian Greenwich Village, they take Halloween to the extreme. The annual Halloween parade displays New York at its craziest *(on 6th Ave.*

between Spring and 21st Sts., www.halloween-nyc.com, starts at 7PM).

Macy's Thanksgiving Day Parade (November)—Giant balloons, marching bands from around the country, and the arrival of Santa! A New York tradition since 1924, the parade steps off at 77th St. and Central Park West, then continues down Broadway all the way to Macy's flagship store in Herald Square at 34th Street *(www.macysparade.com).* If you're not up for the parade, watch them inflate the giant balloons the night before, along Central Park West *(77th/81st Sts., usually from 3:00PM to 10:00PM).*

New York City Marathon (early November)—Each year, about 85,000 runners from around the world wind their way through all five boroughs, to the big finish in Central Park. And all along the way, two million people line the streets to cheer them on *(www.ingnyc marathon.org).*

Winter:

Christmas Tree at Rockefeller Center (lighted a week after Thanksgiving at 7PM)—The annual lighting of the Rockefeller Center Christmas Tree marks the official start of the holiday season. Carefully chosen following a nationwide search (they even transported one from Ottawa, Canada, in 1966), the Norway Spruce (65 to 90 feet tall) is brought to Rockefeller Plaza in November, trimmed, and lighted in a gala ceremony the week after Thanksgiving. While at Rockefeller Center, strap on some skates and show your stuff at the **Rockefeller Center Ice Rink** *(Fifth to Sixth Aves., 49th/50th Sts., 212-332-7654, www.rockefellercenter.com).*

George Balanchine's The Nutcracker™ (November–January)—E.T.A. Hoffmann's classic tale comes to life with George Balanchine's magical production of the *Nutcracker* performed by the **New York City Ballet** *(Lincoln Center, 212-870-5570, www.nycballet.com).*

Radio City Christmas Spectacular (November–January)—Rockettes fill the stage for this annual high-kicking Christmas performance, which has been celebrated for over 75 years *(Radio City Music Hall, 6th Ave., 50/51st Sts., 212-307-1000, www.radiocity.com).*

New Year's Eve Ball Drop (December 31st)—Ring in the new year in Times Square with its infamous ball-dropping countdown. You'll be showered with confetti and cheers. Just be prepared to get intimate with your neighbors—quarters are tight, and security's even tighter *(Times Square, 43rd/Broadway, check Web site for street entrances: www.timessquarenyc.org).*

NEW YORK'S TOP PICKS

New York offers an abundance of one-of-a-kind attractions and experiences for visitors. Here are 13 of the top picks not to be missed!

- ★ Ellis Island *(see page 21)*
- ★ Statue of Liberty *(see page 21)*
- ★ South Street Seaport *(see page 24)*
- ★ Brooklyn Bridge *(see page 37)*
- ★ **Chinatown** *(see page 41)*
- ★ **Times Square** *(see page 114)*
- ★ Empire State Building *(see page 136)*
- ★ Rockefeller Center *(see page 137)*
- ★ St. Patrick's Cathedral *(see page 138)*
- ★ Grand Central Terminal *(see page 139)*
- ★ Museum of Modern Art (MoMA) *(see page 140)*
- ★ Metropolitan Museum of Art *(see page 176)*
- ★ **Central Park** *(see page 185)*

chapter 1

FINANCIAL DISTRICT
BATTERY PARK CITY
TRIBECA
CIVIC CENTER

FINANCIAL DISTRICT
BATTERY PARK CITY
TRIBECA
CIVIC CENTER

Places to See:
1. Wall Street
2. Trinity Church
3. New York Stock Exchange
4. St. Paul's Chapel
5. Ground Zero
6. Bowling Green
7. Battery Park/Ferries
8. Wall Street Bull
9. National Museum of the American Indian
10. New York City Police Museum
11. ELLIS ISLAND ★
12. STATUE OF LIBERTY ★
13. Staten Island Ferry/Whitehall Ferry Terminal
14. South Street Seaport Museum
15. Fraunces Tavern Museum
26. Waterfront
27. North Cove Yacht Harbor
28. Winter Garden/World Financial Center
29. Museum of Jewish Heritage
30. Esplanade
31. Rockefeller Park
32. Robert F. Wagner, Jr. Park
36. Duane Park
37. New York Mercantile Exchange Building
38. apexart
39. Soho Photo Gallery
40. Tribeca Performing Arts Center
56. City Hall
57. Municipal Building
58. Woolworth Building
59. BROOKLYN BRIDGE ★

Places to Eat & Drink:
16. McDonald's
17. Harry's Cafe and Steak
18. Delmonico's
19. Heartland Brewery & Barbeque
20. Carmine's Italian Seafood Restaurant
21. The Full Shilling
22. Fino Wall St. Ristorante
33. Terry's Deli

★ *Top Picks*

Chicago, Boston, Detroit,
they're all the same,
except New York…
that is a city!

—*Eve Minard, in* For Me and My Gal *(1942)*

FINANCIAL DISTRICT

4 5 *to Wall St.;* **2 3** *to Wall St.*

• SNAPSHOT •

Manhattan Island was settled by Europeans, moving south to north, so the oldest neighborhoods are here in what is called Lower Manhattan. At the southern tip is Battery Park, one of New York's oldest public open spaces. More than four million people annually visit the park and its major landmark, Castle Clinton National Monument. Wall Street—so named for the defensive wall that stood here when this area was a Dutch town in the 1600s—and the adjacent financial center are now the financial hub of New York. Although this area has become increasingly residential, with more bars, restaurants, and other amenities than ever before, it's still mostly thought of as a place to work.

PLACES TO SEE
Landmarks:

Wall Street (1) runs east of Broadway to South Street, and was originally a wooden wall built by the Dutch marking the city's northernmost edge. Although the city's financial institutions are now spread over a much wider area (especially post 9/11), this district is still the epicenter of the country's finances. Walking west, check out Trinity Church (2) *(Broadway/Wall Sts., 212-602-0800, admission free)*, a beautiful Gothic Revival structure that offers lunchtime concerts *(see www.trinitywallstreet.org for concert details and opening times)*, with its adjacent churchyard where such notables as Alexander Hamilton are buried. The arch temple to Mammon with its columned portico, the New York Stock Exchange (3) *(11 Wall Street, Broad/New Sts.)* unfortunately has been closed to the public since 9/11. Other nearby landmarks are the lovely 18th-century St. Paul's Chapel (4) *(209 Broadway, Fulton/Vesey Sts., 212-233-4164, www.saint paulschapel.org; hours: M–Sa 10AM–5:45PM, Su 9AM– 3:45PM)*, which houses George Washington's original pew, and, of course, Ground Zero (5) *(Liberty/Vesey Sts., west of Church St.)*, former site of the World Trade Center towers. The **Tribute NYC Visitor Center** *(120 Liberty St., Greenwich/Church Sts., 212-393-9160, www.tributewtc.org; hours: M 10AM–6PM, Tu 12PM– 6PM, W–Sa 10AM–6PM, Su 12PM–5PM))* features exhibits about the Twin Towers and walking tours of the site. Farther south are two oases of green amid the canyons, tiny Bowling Green (6) at the foot of Broadway and Battery Park (7) *(south of Battery Place)*, where the ferries (7) to Ellis Island and the Statue of Liberty depart *(see "Arts & Entertainment," which follows)*.

Arts & Entertainment:

At Bowling Green (6), you'll find the famous bronze statue of the Wall Street Bull (8). Also at Bowling Green is the National Museum of the American Indian (9) *(1 Bowling Green, State/Whitehall Sts., 212-514-3700, www.nmai.si.edu, free admission; hours: daily 10AM–5PM, Thu until 8PM)*, housed in the Beaux Arts former U.S. Custom House Building. The collection features thousands of works from textiles to carved stone heads. And the building itself, with its painted ceilings and great atrium, is worth the visit alone. The **New York City Police Museum (10)** *(100 Old Slip, Water/South Sts., 212-480-3100, www.nycpolicemuseum.org; hours: M–Sa 10AM–5PM)*, with its re-created crime scenes, complete with chalk body outlines and fake drug stashes, is more than a little hokey, but it's also one of the city's most charming and fascinating small museums. Take a **ferry** from **Battery Park (7):** Buy ferry tickets to ★**ELLIS ISLAND (11)** *(see below)*, with its wonderful immigration museum, or the ★**STATUE OF LIBERTY (12)** *(see below)* on Liberty Island, both from Castle Clinton National Monument, a circular sandstone fort in Battery Park *(for advance tickets call 866-782-8834)*. The ancestors of almost half of today's Americans entered the country through ★**ELLIS ISLAND (11)** *(212-363-3200, www.nps.gov/elis; hours: daily 9AM–5PM, closed Dec. 25th)*. More than 12 million new Americans passed through this immigration portal from 1892 to 1954. Visitors get a taste of the real experience by walking through the Baggage Room (where the immigrants would first arrive and drop off their belongings), or sitting in the Registry Room. There are also interactive audio exhibits where you can hear immigrants speak of their experiences passing through Ellis Island. In addition, visitors can learn about the island's rich past and research their own family's immigration history. You are also welcome to get up close to the ★**STATUE OF LIBERTY (12)** *(212-363-3200, www.nps.gov/stli; hours:*

daily 9:30AM–5PM, closed Dec. 25th), which greeted most of those newcomers arriving through Ellis Island. Standing as tall as a 22-story building, she has guarded New York Harbor since 1886. A gift of friendship from France, she is an international symbol of freedom. Photographs, oral histories, prints, and videos are displayed on the 2nd floor. They cover the history and symbolism of the statue throughout the years. You can also take the free Staten Island Ferry (13)—the city's best bargain—to Staten Island and back from the contemporary glass Whitehall Ferry Terminal (13) *(end of Whitehall St. at the water, 718-815-BOAT, www.siferry.com).* The South Street Seaport Museum (14) *(Visitors' Center: 12 Fulton St. at South St., 212-748-8600, www.southstreetseaport museum.org; hours: January–March galleries Th–Su 10AM–5PM, ships open 10AM–4PM; April–December galleries and ships open Tu–Su 10AM–6PM)* has a great collection of old sailing ships lining the dock, offering tours inside, plus a museum with frequently changing exhibits. The Fraunces Tavern Museum (15) *(54 Pearl St. at corner of Broad St., 212-425-1778, www.fraunces tavernmuseum.org; hours: M–Sa 12PM–5PM)* opened to the public in 1907. The original tavern was a meeting ground for the Sons of Liberty in the pre-revolutionary years, and became the site in which Washington gave his farewell speech at the end of the war.

Kids:

The South Street Seaport Museum (14) has programs for kids and families. Check out "Family Programs" on its Web site, www.southstreetseaportmuseum.org, for details. Amid the cobblestone streets of the seaport, there are also plenty of street performers drawing crowds and needing young volunteers for spectacular stunts and magic tricks. Take your kids on a ferry to see "Lady Liberty" up close. Buy tickets at Castle Clinton in Battery Park (7) *(see page 21)*. And if you have young aspiring crime fighters in your family, they'll enjoy the New York City Police Museum (10) *(see page 21)*.

PLACES TO EAT & DRINK
Where to Eat:

McDonald's (16) ($) *(160 Broadway, just north of Wall St., 212-385-2063; daily 24 hours)*. Yes, McDonald's. Befitting its tony locale, this one has a doorman, a pianist, and waitress service.

Harry's Cafe and Steak (17) ($$) *(1 Hanover Sq. at Pearl St., 212-785-9200, www.harrysnyc. com; hours: M–Sa 11:30AM–12AM)* is a classic steakhouse noted for its aged strip steaks and worthy wine cellar. Delmonico's (18) ($$$$) *(56 Beaver St. at South William St., 212-509-1144, www.delmonicosny.com; hours: M–F 11:30AM–10PM, Sa 5PM–10PM)* offers classic American fare in a classic 19th-century building. **Heartland Brewery & Barbeque (19) ($$)** *(93 South St. at Fulton St., 646-572-2337, www.heartlandbrewery.com; hours: M–F 11:30AM–9PM, Sa–Su 11:30AM–10PM)* is a mini-chain that's good for beers 'n' burgers basics in a nice corner space.

Carmine's Italian Seafood Restaurant (20) ($$) *(140 Beekman St. at Front St., 212-962-8606, www.carminesat theseaport.com; hours: M–Th, Su 12PM–10PM, F 12PM– 11PM, Sa 1PM–11PM)* is a real slice of old New York. This former Mafia hangout just yards from the bustling seaport has been in operation for more than 100 years, yet is unknown to most tourists. Enjoy fresh seafood and drinks at its ancient bar and battered wooden booths. The calamari's great.

Bars & Nightlife:

The Full Shilling (21) *(160 Pearl St., Wall/Pine Sts., 212-422-3855, www.thefullshilling.com; hours: daily 12PM– 12AM)* is worth going to for the décor alone—a genuine-imported-from-Ireland antique bar that puts any patron in a drinking frame of mind. There is a good selection of beers and comfort food, too. **Fino Wall St. Ristorante (22)** *(1 Wall St. at Pearl St., 212-825-1924, www.finony.com; hours: M–F 12PM–10PM)* is about eating as much as drinking, with its excellent Northern Italian fare and wide range of Italian wines.

WHERE TO SHOP

Don't miss Century 21 (23) *(22 Cortlandt St., Broadway/ Church St., 212-227-9092, www.c21stores.com; hours: M–W 7:45AM–9PM, Th–F 7:45AM–9:30PM, Sa 10AM– 9PM, Su 11AM–8PM)*, a department store stuffed with designer clothes for kids and adults at low prices. There's also plenty of shopping at and around the ★SOUTH STREET SEAPORT (24) *(Pier 17 and environs, South Street to the East River, Fletcher/*

TOP PICK!

Beekman Sts., www.southstreetseaport.com; mall hours: M–Sa 10AM–7PM, Su 11AM–6PM; restaurants and bars have extended hours), from the Body Shop and Ann Taylor to gadget store Brookstone. Sports fans revel at the N.Y. Yankees Clubhouse Shop. Teens fall into Abercrombie & Fitch. This historic venue boasts more than 100 stores and eateries (Nathan's Famous Hot Dogs, anyone?) and some of the best views of the East River and the Brooklyn Bridge. While visiting, be sure to get your fill of New York nautical history at the South Street Seaport Museum (14) *(see page 22)*.

WHERE TO STAY

The Wall Street Inn (25) ($$-$$$) *(9 South William St. at Broad St., 212-747-1500, www.thewallstreetinn.com)* is a stylish if fairly basic hotel in a neighborhood otherwise given over to efficient but soulless corporate hospitality.

BATTERY PARK CITY

1 *to Chambers St., Rector St.;* **2 3** *to Chambers St.*

● SNAPSHOT ●

Along the Hudson River and west of the financial district is Battery Park City, a mini-metropolis built on landfill that, in typical New York fashion, nestles right next to the most historic part of the city. The Esplanade is one of the star attractions of Battery Park City. Its wide pathways give pedestrians key access to the river. In the midst of this residential neighborhood lies its commercial side: the World Financial Center and Winter Garden.

PLACES TO SEE
Landmarks:

The best thing about Battery Park City (east of the Hudson River from Battery Place to Chambers St.) is its wonderful waterfront (26), part of a Hudson River Greenway that runs as far north as Harlem. There are spaces to jog, walk, rollerblade, or just sit back and relax, all with amazing views of Jersey City's towers across the water. During warmer months there are always free cul-

tural events *(see www.batteryparkcity.org for details)*. The yachts moored in the North Cove Yacht Harbor (27) *(waterfront between Vesey/Liberty Sts.)* are worth ogling. The Winter Garden (28) is a glorious 10-story glass atrium with palm trees, food courts, and shopping, plus views of the Hudson and Jersey shores. It is located in the **World Financial Center (28)** plaza *(see "Where to Shop," page 29)*, which has numerous restaurants and shops, and hosts many (often free) musical and other events *(see www.worldfinancialcenter.com for details)*.

Arts & Entertainment:

The ziggurat-shaped **Museum of Jewish Heritage (29)** *(Robert F. Wagner, Jr. Park, 36 Battery Pl. at First Pl., 646-437-4200, www.mjhnyc.org; hours: Su–Tu, Th 10AM–5:45PM; W 10AM–8PM; F 10AM–5PM; eve of Jewish holidays 10AM–3PM)*, located in the southern end of Battery Park City, is a relative newcomer, but well worth the visit. It's packed with photographs and objects documenting the past 100 years of Jewish life and is also a living memorial to the Holocaust. The surrounding park and nearby landscaped walkways make for a lovely outside stroll.

Kids:

Battery Park City is one of the most child-friendly places in the city and is so well-designed that adults can enjoy it equally—something that can't be said about a lot of children's attractions. The big draw here is the beautiful 1.2-mile **Esplanade (30)** that runs along the Hudson River from Chambers Street to Battery Place and offers amazing views of the Statue of Liberty, Ellis Island, and the Jersey City waterfront. Along the Esplanade are numerous small parks for children, adults, and even dogs. For toddlers, the best one is the **Rockefeller Park (31)** *(near Chambers St.)*, which contains the Real World

Sculpture Garden, filled with wonderful little bronze sculptures by artist Tom Otterness. There's also a wading fountain to cool off on those hot NYC summer days. The **Robert F. Wagner, Jr. Park (32)** *(southern tip of Battery Park City, south of the Museum of Jewish Heritage)* is also particularly good for young children. It has clean, safe bathrooms, sprinklers in the summer, water tables, and more.

PLACES TO EAT & DRINK
Where to Eat:

Battery Park City is not exactly the most renowned place for eating out, to put it mildly, though there are a number of restaurants both inside the **Winter Garden (28)** atrium and lining the plaza outside (which offer amazing views over the Hudson River). If you're strolling around, your best bet is to try a couple of locals' favorites for take-out. **Terry's Deli (33) ($)** *(410 W. Chambers St. at North End Ave., 212-267-2816; hours: M–Su 7AM–12AM)* has good, if basic, sandwiches and the like, and **Lili's Noodle Shop & Grill (34) ($)** *(102 North End Ave., near Vesey St., 212-786-1300; hours: Su–Th 11AM–10:30PM, F–Sa 12PM–11:30PM)* offers great egg rolls.

WHERE TO SHOP

The **World Financial Center (28)** has a host of stores and specialty shops to suit all of your needs—from fine cigars to chocolates to designer clothes for men and women.

WHERE TO STAY

The **New York Marriott Financial Center (35) ($$$-$$$$)** *(85 West St., Albany/Carlisle Sts., 212-385-4900, www. nycmarriottfinancial.com)* comes with all the bells and whistles you'd expect, including a fancy restaurant, Internet access in each room, and fancy harbor views.

TRIBECA

❶ to Canal St., Franklin St. or Chambers St.; ❷❸ to Chambers St.; Ⓐ Ⓒ Ⓔ to Canal St.

● SNAPSHOT ●

Tribeca used to be the site of Washington Market, a major distribution center for meat, produce, and dairy products. The warehouses and store-and-loft buildings

here date from the 19th and early 20th centuries. After the market moved to the Bronx, the neighborhood was slowly transformed into a residential one. It now offers some of the best eating, drinking, and architecture in the city.

PLACES TO SEE
Landmarks:

Tribeca is home to some of the most flamboyant creations in stone and brick, each vying to outdo the other. **Duane Park (36)** *(Hudson, Duane, and Staple Sts.)* is a delightful triangular pocket, surrounded by cast-iron buildings that were still home to remnants of the city's dairy produce industry until the late 1970s. The **New York Mercantile Exchange Building (37)** *(6 Harrison St., Greenwich/Hudson Sts.)* has a fantastic red brick façade, complete with clock face. Once home to the dairy trade's equivalent of the stock exchange, it has been handsomely restored.

Arts & Entertainment:

Tribeca has also become famous in recent years for resident Robert DeNiro's annual **Tribeca Film Festival** *(www.tribecafilmfestival.org for details)*, held in various neighborhood locations at the end of April. Some think it has become too mainstream in recent years (its attendance has surpassed 300,000 in previous years), but if you're into star-gazing, then this is the place to be each spring. Since its inception in 1994, **apexart (38)** *(291 Church St., White/Walker Sts., 212-431-5270, www.apexart.org; hours: Tu–Sa 11AM–6PM)* has been know for its unpredictable, and innovative exhibits. More than 1,200 artists have participated in their wide variety of shows. They also host a number of special programs and events, including artist lectures and roundtable discussions. The **Soho Photo Gallery (39)** *(15 White St., West Broadway/Church St., 212-226-8571, www.sohophoto.com: W–Su 1PM–6PM or by appointment)* is one of the numerous galleries that dot Tribeca. Established in 1971 as a non-profit run by a large number of photographers, it offers a dozen or so different shows a year. The Soho name remains, but the gallery relocated to Tribeca in 1979.

Kids:

From October to June the **Tribeca Performing Arts Center (40)** *(199 Chambers St., Greenwich St./West Side Highway, 212-220-1460, www.tribecapac.org)* offers a mixed bag of puppet, theater, and musical shows for children aged 3 and up. If you want to eat out with your children, **Edward's (41) ($)** *(136 West Broadway, Thomas/Duane Sts., 212-233-6436, www.edwardsnyc.com; hours: breakfast*

M–F 9AM–11AM, Sa–Su 9AM–10AM; brunch Sa–Su 10AM–5PM; lunch daily 11AM–5PM; dinner daily 5PM–12AM) offers a handy combination of hip interior for Mom and Dad plus child-friendly waitstaff who can serve up special kids' menu items of fish sticks and the like.

PLACES TO EAT & DRINK
Where to Eat:

Tribeca has some of the most famous restaurants in the city, and you'd be well advised to call in advance to get a table at some of them. For top-end French dining there's **Bouley (42) ($$$$)** *(163 Duane St. at Hudson St., 212-964-2525, www.davidbouley.com; hours: lunch daily 11:30AM–3PM; dinner daily 5PM–11:30PM)*, where Chef David Bouley infuses his flair for tropical flavors with his French grandmother's inspired cooking traditions. Jackets are preferred, but not required. If you like Japanese food, try **Nobu (43) ($$$)** *(105 Hudson St. at Franklin St., 212-219-0500, www.myriadrestaurantgroup.com; hours: M–F 11:45AM–2:15PM, M–Su 5:45PM–10:15PM)*, chef Nobu Matsuhisa's temple to fish where, if you're lucky enough to get in, you will undoubtedly encounter some of the best people-watching in the city. It isn't hip, but if you want a quiet supper with that special someone in an elegant, high-ceilinged space where you can hear yourself talk, **Capsouto Frères (44) ($$)** *(451 Washington St., Desbrosses/Watts Sts., 212-966-4900, www.capsoutofreres. com; hours: lunch Tu–F 12PM–3:30PM; dinner M–F 6PM–10:30PM, Sa–Su 6PM–11:30PM; brunch Sa–Su*

12PM–3:30PM) is the place to go. The food is French-American, and one of the Capsouto brothers will probably drop by your table. The restaurant is in a beautiful brick and stone building that was once a warehouse. For much more casual lunches and dinners, there's always that reliable old standard **Odeon (45) ($$)** *(145 West Broadway at Duane St., 212-233-0507, www.theodeonrestaurant. com; hours: lunch M–F 11:45AM–3PM; dinner daily 5:30PM–12AM; brasserie menu Sa–Su 4PM–5:30PM, M–W 12AM–1AM, Th–Sa 12AM–2AM; brunch Sa–Su 10AM–4PM)*, a French bistro whose fries and warm mahogany paneling combine for a dining experience as soothing as a warm bath. If you're more into a casual brunch or snack-and-run, there's **Bubby's Pie Company (46) ($)** *(120 Hudson St. at N. Moore St., 212-219-0666, www.bubbys.com; hours: M–Th 8AM–11PM, F 8AM–12AM, Sa 6PM–12AM, Su 6PM–10PM, brunch Sa–Su 9AM–4PM)*, a corner joint that has grown into an institution and is packed on weekends.

Bars & Nightlife:

If you want something a little upmarket, Tribeca is the home of the sophisticated watering hole. **Anotheroom (47)** *(249 W. Broadway, 212-226-1418, www.theotheroom.com; hours: Su–M 5PM–2AM, Tu–Sa 5PM–4AM)* has been declared a great date bar. The owners of The Room and The Otheroom stock this, their Tribeca outlet, with a wide selection of Eurobrews and domestic beers that change with the seasons. **Walker's (48)** *(16 N. Moore St. at Varick St., 212-941-0142; hours: daily*

11AM–4AM) is a dying breed in this neighborhood—a classic, old-time bar where you can sip pints and chat in a friendly, utterly unpretentious atmosphere, and if you get hungry pop around to its long back room for above-average burgers, fries, and the like.

WHERE TO SHOP

If Deco is your thing, Antiqueria Tribeca (49) *(129 Duane St., West Broadway/Church Sts., 212-227-7500, www.antiqueria.com; hours: M 10AM–5PM, Tu–Sa 11AM–6PM)* has tons of it, as well as other 20th-century European furnishings and objets d'art, all housed in a landmarked building. Store owner Ann Ljungberg brings Scandinavian design to New York at the stylish and chic Just Scandinavian (50) *(161 Hudson St., at Laight St., 212-334-2556, www.justscandinavian.com; hours: Tu–F 10AM–6PM, Sa–Su 12PM–6PM).* The store is a treasure trove of home accessories and furnishings that are colorful, fresh, and functional. Issey Miyake (51) *(119 Hudson St., Franklin/N. Moore Sts., 212-226-0100, www.tribecaisseymiyake.com; hours: M–Sa, 11AM–7PM, Su 12PM–6PM)* is a suitably amazing space (it's designed by architect Frank Gehry) for Miyake's amazing men's and women's clothes. This sculptural chic will set you

back, though. At Shoofly (52) *(42 Hudson St., Duane/ Thomas Sts., 212-406-3270, www.shooflynyc.com; hours: M–Sa 10AM–7PM, Su 12PM–6PM),* with its lovely European (mostly) children's clothes, you can indulge your parental fantasies about what your little darlings really should look like. **Archipelago (53)** *(38 Walker St., Broadway/Church St., 212-334-9460, www. archipelagoinc.com; hours: M–F 9:30AM–5:30PM)* is a must for high-thread-count addicts; it offers an enormous selection of linens, bedsheets, napkins, and more.

WHERE TO STAY

For visitors, Tribeca is a playground rather than a place to stay, though if you've got the money, the ultra-sleek 203-room boutique hotel, the **Tribeca Grand (54) ($$$$)** *(2 Avenue of the Americas, White/Walker Sts., 212-519-6600, www.tribecagrand.com)*, is not a bad place to rest your head. A bonus of staying here is that the concierge can often get you a table at some of the tougher local restaurants to crack. More modestly, there's the 125-room **Cosmopolitan Hotel (55) ($$)** *(95 West Broadway at Chambers St., 888-895-9400, www.cosmohotel.com)*, which costs about a third of the price of the Grand and lacks its luxury design, but is one of the city's genuine bargains.

CIVIC CENTER

4 **5** **6** *to Brooklyn Bridge-City Hall;*
R *to City Hall;* **J** **Z** *to Chambers St.*

● SNAPSHOT ●

When this area was first built up, it marked the northern edge of the city. When City Hall was being built in 1803, the northern façade of the building was left unfinished because no one thought the city would expand farther north. As was true then, this is where the city government resides. There are a number of imposing, majestic public buildings here. The Woolworth Building was the tallest building in the world from 1913 to 1929, until an uptown rival rose higher.

PLACES TO SEE
Landmarks:

City Hall (56), from which the mayor runs this vast megalopolis, is a white Renaissance creation dating from 1812, set amid lovely gardens with fountains *(Vesey to Chambers Sts., Broadway to Park Row)*. City Hall and the immediate area are closed to the public, but the southern parts of the gardens are open to all. Across from it is the Municipal Building (57) *(1 Centre St. opposite Chambers St.)*, with its magnificent colonnade. Upstairs is the public marriage office and chapel, which is both an amusing and genuinely touching place to visit. The most striking building by far is the classic Woolworth Building (58) *(233 Broadway, Park Place/Barclay St.)*—a

Gothic masterpiece rising 792 feet, and the tallest building in the world when it opened in 1913. ★**BROOKLYN BRIDGE (59)** *(entrance near Park Row)* is one of the world's most recognizable and beautiful bridges. This steel and granite span was the longest suspension bridge when it was built in 1883, connecting Manhattan with Brooklyn (which was a separate city before the bridge was built). It makes for a wonderful walk (or ride—bikers on the right, pedestrians on the left) over the East River, offering beautiful views of Manhattan.

TOP PICK!

PLACES TO EAT & DRINK
Where to Eat:

This area caters to a busy brown-bag grabbing workforce during the day. Your best bet is to slip off north and east to Chinatown, or west to Tribeca. If you do want to stay in the area for a quick bite, try **Fulton Street (60)** or **Beekman Street (61)**, where you'll find a variety of small, family-run delicatessens.

WHERE TO SHOP

One word rules here: electronics. Over the years, the family-owned J&R Music and Computer World (62) *(15-23 Park Row, Ann/Beekman Sts., 212-238-9000, www.jr.com; hours: M–Sa 9AM–7:30PM, Su 10:30AM–6:30PM)* has expanded to cover virtually all the southern end of Park Row. Cameras, DVDs, computers, CDs—these guys have it all at cheap prices, and are renowned for their friendliness and expertise.

chapter 2

Gothic masterpiece rising 792 feet, and the tallest building in the world when it opened in 1913. ★BROOKLYN BRIDGE (59) *(entrance near Park Row)* is one of the world's most recognizable and beautiful bridges. This steel and granite span was the longest suspension bridge when it was built in 1883, connecting Manhattan with Brooklyn (which was a separate city before the bridge was built). It makes for a wonderful walk (or ride—bikers on the right, pedestrians on the left) over the East River, offering beautiful views of Manhattan.

TOP PICK!

PLACES TO EAT & DRINK
Where to Eat:

This area caters to a busy brown-bag grabbing workforce during the day. Your best bet is to slip off north and east to Chinatown, or west to Tribeca. If you do want to stay in the area for a quick bite, try **Fulton Street (60)** or **Beekman Street (61)**, where you'll find a variety of small, family-run delicatessens.

WHERE TO SHOP

One word rules here: electronics. Over the years, the family-owned J&R Music and Computer World (62) *(15-23 Park Row, Ann/Beekman Sts., 212-238-9000, www.jr.com; hours: M–Sa 9AM–7:30PM, Su 10:30AM–6:30PM)* has expanded to cover virtually all the southern end of Park Row. Cameras, DVDs, computers, CDs—these guys have it all at cheap prices, and are renowned for their friendliness and expertise.

chapter 2

CHINATOWN
LITTLE ITALY & NOLITA
LOWER EAST SIDE
EAST VILLAGE

Places to See:

1. Eastern States Buddhist Temple
2. 130 Bowery
3. The Forward Building
4. Columbus Park
5. Museum of the Chinese in the Americas
19. Saint Patrick's Old Cathedral
20. Umberto's Clam House
21. Police Building Apartments
22. Feast of San Gennaro
39. Lower East Side Tenement Museum
40. Eldridge Street Synagogue
41. The Living Room
42. ABC No Rio
43. Landmark's Sunshine Cinema
60. Nicholas and Elizabeth Stuyvesant Fish House
61. 151 Avenue B
62. New York City Marble Cemetery
63. Grace Church
64. Tompkins Square Park
65. Cooper Union
66. La MaMa E.T.C.
67. St. Mark's-in-the-Bowery Church
68. Bowery Poetry Club
69. KGB
70. Nuyorican Poets Café
71. Theater for the New City
72. St. Mark's Place
73. GRNY
74. Michael Mut Gallery
75. First Street Playground

Places to Eat & Drink:

6. Original Chinatown Ice Cream Factory
7. N.Y. Noodle Town
8. Fuleen Seafood Restaurant
9. XO Kitchen
10. Joe's Shanghai Restaurant
11. Ping's Seafood
12. Nha Trang
13. Vegetarian Dim Sum House
23. Café Napoli
24. Café Gitane

Where to Shop:

Where to Stay:

CHINATOWN

6 to Canal St.; **N R Q** to Canal St.;
B D to Grand St.; **J Z** to Canal-Centre Sts.

● SNAPSHOT ●

With its winding alleyways, open air markets, street vendors, Chinese signs, and crowds haggling in Cantonese
over seafood so fresh it's still swimming in the
tank, ★**CHINATOWN** has an old-fashioned
and exotic urban atmosphere that makes it
one of the favorite destinations for New
Yorkers and tourists alike. Over the years Chinatown's
boundaries have spread, eating into nearby Little Italy so
there's barely a rump of it left. This expansion continues
today as endless waves of Asian immigrants continue to
pour into what is the largest Asian community outside
Asia. With its crowded streets and high-speed pace, the
atmosphere is always electric in Chinatown.

TOP PICK!

PLACES TO SEE
Landmarks:

Check out the rows of gleaming golden Buddha statues
at the **Eastern States Buddhist Temple (1)** *(64 Mott St.,
Canal/Bayard Sts., 212-966-6229; hours: daily 9AM–
6PM)*. The **Forward Building (3)** *(173-175 East Broadway,
Rutgers/Jefferson Sts.,)* is an intriguing symbol of the con-
tinuing growth and vitality of Chinatown. Once the
headquarters of a famous Yiddish newspaper, it is now a
residential property. In nice weather, the locals play

mah-jongg (a Chinese game using up to 144 tiles and played with four people) and practice *tai chi* in **Columbus Park (4)** *(Baxter, Bayard, and Mulberry Sts.)*.

Arts & Entertainment:

With its amazing cultural diversity, New York hosts many different ethnic and cultural events, but few come close to the extravaganza of the **Chinese New Year**, celebrated every February during a two-week period (the date changes slightly each year) with firecrackers, a huge procession with dancing dragons that snakes in and out of various restaurants, and of course masses of delicious food. It's centered on Mott Street *(call Official NYC Information Center at 212-484-1222 for details)* but includes a number of locations. The **Museum of the Chinese in the Americas (MoCA) (5)** *(215 Centre St., Howard/Grand, 212-619-4785, www.mocanyc.org; hours: M–W, F 11AM–5PM, Th 11AM–9PM, Sa–Su 10AM–5PM)* is a little-known cultural attraction, but one definitely worth visiting. Set discreetly inside an old school building, it offers not only excellent temporary exhibitions, but also a permanent collection of artifacts, letters, and remarkable photographs documenting the lives of Chinese immigrants to this country.

Kids:

The **Chinese New Year** *(212-484-1222, www.nycvisit. com)*, with its firecrackers and dragon costumes, is fun for older kids if you're here in February, though toddlers might be scared. Kids (and adults!) of all ages will enjoy a treat from the **Original Chinatown Ice Cream Factory (6)** *(65 Bayard St., Mott/Elizabeth Sts., 212-608-4170,* *www.chinatownicecreamfactory.com; hours: daily 11AM–10PM)*. They give the popular American dessert an exotic Chinese twist with their range of flavors such as lychee, ginger, red bean, and zen butter. But if you're not feeling that adventurous, they've got all the classics too!

PLACES TO EAT & DRINK
Where to Eat:

Chinatown has great street food. Vendors selling freshly cooked noodles, pancakes, and other Asian specialties park their carts up and down Canal Street. Any vendor who has a long line of customers waiting is a good bet. The budget traveler can eat very well here, but remember to bring cash: many restaurants do not accept credit cards. Although you can never choose wrong simply by looking in the windows and deciding where the Chinese eat, some reliable standards are these: **N.Y. Noodle Town (7) ($)** *(28-1/2 Bowery at Bayard St., 212-349-0923, cash only; hours: daily 9AM–4AM)* for—what else?—scrumptious noodles at a very low price. Fresh fish swimming in their tanks will greet you at **Fuleen Seafood Restaurant (8) ($$)** *(11 Division St., near Bowery, 212-941-6888, www.fuleen restaurant.com; hours: daily 11AM–2:30AM)*. **XO Kitchen (9) ($)** *(148 Hester St., Bowery/Elizabeth St., 212-965-8645, cash only; hours: daily 8AM–11PM)* specializes in the cuisine of Hong Kong. The legendary dumplings at **Joe's Shanghai Restaurant (10) ($–$$)** *(9 Pell St., Mott/Bowery Sts., 212-233-8888, cash only, www.joeshanghairestaurants. com; hours: M–Sa 11AM–11PM)* explain the long line of people usually waiting to get in. But it's worth the wait. Just make sure to first take a nibble into the dumpling, and then "slurp" the soup out to avoid burning your mouth! Fresh seafood and a slightly more upscale atmosphere are the draws of **Ping's Seafood (11) ($$)** *(22 Mott St., Mosco/Pell Sts., 212-602-9988; hours: daily 10AM–11PM)*—a Chinatown favorite. For a change of pace, savor a steamy bowl of pho soup at **Nha Trang (12) ($-$$)** *(148 Centre St., Walker/White Sts., 212-941-9292; hours: daily 10:30AM–10PM)*, a low-key Vietnamese choice. The setting is minimal, but the menu is huge at the **Vegetarian Dim Sum House (13) ($)** *(24 Pell St., Mott/Bowery Sts., 212-577-7176; hours: 10:30AM–10:30PM daily)*.

WHERE TO SHOP

Pick up a genuine pair of chopsticks from Yunhong Chopsticks Shop (14) *(50 Mott St., at Bayard St., 212-566-8828, www.happychopsticks.com; hours: daily 10:30AM–8PM)*. Chinatown is a popular destination for bargain hunters. **Canal Street**, especially, is lined with shops selling cheap knockoff designer watches and gold jewelry. Stop in at Kam Man Food Products (15) *(200 Canal St. at Mulberry St., 212-571-0330, hours: daily 8:30AM–8:45PM)* for everything from dried jellyfish to cookware. Mott Street (16) is a good place to pick up cheap souvenirs like Chinese children's pajamas, beaded slippers, and bits of jade. If you're interested in alternative medicine, stop in at the Ten Ren Tea & Ginseng Co. (17) *(75 Mott St., Canal/Bayard Sts., 212-349-2286, www.tenrenusa.com; hours: Su–Th 11AM–9PM, F–Sa 11AM–10PM)*. You'll find Eastern teapots, flowerpots, and more at the New Jade Garden Crafts (18) *(76 Mulberry St., Canal/Bayard Sts., 212-587-5685; hours: daily 10AM–7PM)*.

B D F M *to Broadway-Lafayette;*
N R *to Prince St.;* **6** *to Spring St.*

• SNAPSHOT •

Since most of the immigrants (and their descendants) who once lived on or around Mulberry Street have moved out to other Italian neighborhoods or the 'burbs, the enclave of Little Italy is just a shadow of its former self. The crowds still come, however, to enjoy the restaurants, cafes, groceries, and the week-long Feast of San Gennaro every September. Nolita (North of Little Italy) is a relatively new neighborhood, home to one-of-a-kind boutiques for the young and fashionable.

PLACES TO SEE
Landmarks:

Probably the most beautiful spot in the neighborhood is **Saint Patrick's Old Cathedral (19)** *(263 Mulberry St., Houston/Prince Sts., 212-226-8075, www.oldsaint patricks.com; rectory hours M–F 8AM–5PM)*. Built 1809–1815 in a Gothic Revival style, it's the oldest Catholic Church in the city. **Umberto's Clam House (20)** *(178 Mulberry St. at Broome St., 212-431-7545, www. umbertosclamhouse.com; hours: daily 11AM–4AM)*, a very different historic landmark, is where Joey Gallo, a famous Mafioso, was shot to death in 1972. The **Police Building Apartments (21)** *(240 Centre St., Grand/Broome Sts.)*, built in 1905–1909, is a handsome Edwardian structure with a huge dome. The police department vacated it in 1973, and 10 years later it was converted into cooperative apartments. Walk over to **130 Bowery (2)** *(130 Bowery, Broome/Grand Sts.)*, designed by the famous New York architecture firm, McKim, Mead & White, in 1893. Its marble Corinthian columns and soaring ceilings won it landmark status in 1966. Previously the Bowery Savings Bank, **130 Bowery (2)** is now home to Capitale, a restaurant and event space.

Arts & Entertainment:

Little Italy's pleasures lie mostly in strolling around its old tenement-lined streets, absorbing its plentiful street life and, of course, sampling its gastronomic delights. But every September Little Italy is host to the **Feast of San Gennaro (22)** *(Mulberry St., Canal/Houston Sts., 212-768-9320, www.sangennaro.org)*, a huge tourist attraction with endless food vendors lining the streets, and a Ferris wheel and other sideshow pleasures imported. Many New Yorkers avoid it like the plague, considering its charms to have vanished long ago, but there's no denying that at night, with the streets all lit up, it can be a romantic sight.

Kids:

Italy is famous for its child-indulging culture, and kids are welcome in most of Little Italy's restaurants, though it's quite an urban area and otherwise not of the greatest interest to most young ones. If you're here in September, the **Feast of San Gennaro (22)** *(see page 46)* will probably hold their attention most. **Café Napoli (23)** *(191*

Hester St. at Mulberry St., 212-226-8705; hours: daily 9AM–3PM) lets you take your time demolishing your plate of pasta and offers children's portions as well.

PLACES TO EAT & DRINK
Where to Eat:

Café Gitane (24) ($) *(242 Mott St., Houston/Prince Sts., 212-334-9552; hours: Su–Th 9AM–12AM, F–Sa 9AM–12:30AM)*, right across the street from St. Patrick's, is a good place to sit, sip mint tea, nibble reasonably priced Moroccan specialties, and gaze on the church with its peaceful, tree-shaded cemetery. **Lombardi's (25) ($)** *(32 Spring St., Mott/Mulberry Sts., 212-941-7994, www.firstpizza.com; hours: Su–Th 11:30AM–11PM, F–Sa 11:30AM–12AM)* offers great New York pizza pies (no slices) in a turn-of-the century restaurant. There's

no shortage of pizza places in Little Italy. Try **Pomodoro (26) ($)** *(51 Spring St., at Mulberry St., 212-966-9229;*

hours: M–W 11AM–11PM, Th–Sa 11AM–4AM, Su 11AM–10PM) for the best vodka pizza you've ever tasted. Comfort food abounds at **Nolita House (27) ($$)** (47 E. Houston St., Mott/Mulberry Sts., 212-625-1712, www.nolitahouse.com; hours: M 11:30AM–3:30PM, 5PM–10PM, Tu–F 11:30AM–3:30PM, 5PM–11PM, Sa 10AM–4PM, 5PM–11PM, Su 10AM–4PM, 5PM–10PM). **Café Colonial (28) ($-$$)** (276 Elizabeth St. at Houston St., 212-274-0044; www.cafecolonialny.com; hours: M–F 10AM–10:30PM, Sa–Su 9AM–11PM) offers Brazilian dishes, salads, and sandwiches, and, in the summer months, outdoor seating. **Peasant (29) ($$-$$$)** (194 Elizabeth St., Prince/Spring Sts., 212-965-9511; www. peasantnyc.com; hours: Tu–Sa 6PM–11PM, Su 6PM–10PM) provides rustic Italian cuisine served in a dim, romantic interior. **Public (30) ($$$)** (210 Elizabeth St., Prince/ Spring Sts., 212-343-7011; www.public-nyc.com; hours: M–Th 6PM–11PM with bar open to 1AM; F–Sa 6PM–12AM with bar open to 2AM; Su 6PM–10:30PM with bar open to 1AM; brunch Sa–Su 11AM–3:30PM) is great if you're tired of Italian and want to join the trendy crowds enjoying Asian fusion cuisine.

Have a cappuccino at the turn of the century **Caffe Roma Pastry (31)** (385 Broome St., Mulberry/Mott Sts., 212-226-8413; hours: daily 8AM–12AM).

Bars & Nightlife:

If you want to feel like a star in your very own *Mean Streets*, **Mulberry Street Bar (32)** (formerly **Mare Chiaro**) *(176 Mulberry St., Broome/Grand Sts., 212-226-9345, cash only; hours: daily Su–Th 11AM–2AM, F–Sa 11AM–3AM)*—an old dark dive complete with phone booth,

photos of the owner posing with what was then a very downtown Madonna—will fit the bill. Order a cheap beer and play some Sinatra on the jukebox.

WHERE TO SHOP

Go to **DiPalo's Fine Foods (33)** *(200 Grand St. at Mott St., 212-226-1033; www.dipaloselects.com; hours: M–Sa 9AM–6:30PM, Su 9AM–4PM)* and the **Italian Food Center (34)** *(186 Grand St. at Mulberry St., 212-925-2954; hours: daily 8AM–9PM)* for olive oil, fresh pasta, and made-on-the-spot hero sandwiches. **Dö Kham (35)** *(51 Prince St., Mott/Mulberry Sts., 212-966-2404; www. dokhamny.com; hours: daily 10AM–8PM)*, a Tibetan shop, has silk stoles, strik-ing silver jewelry, and

stunning fur-lined Tibetan hats. The boutique shop **Only Hearts (36)** *(230 Mott St., Prince/Spring Sts., 212-431-3694, www.onlyhearts.com; hours: M–Sa 12PM–8PM, Su 12PM–7PM)*, has much more to offer than just hearts—from lingerie to dresses you'll find unique and fashionable items to add to your wardrobe. If you're a fashionista on a budget, Ina Nolita (37) *(21 Prince St., Elizabeth/Mott Sts., 212-334-9048, www.inanyc.com; hours: M–Sa 12PM–8PM, Su 12PM–7PM)* is a designer consignment shop. If you have more cash to spare, try Sigerson Morrison (38) *(28 Prince St., Elizabeth/Mott Sts., 212-219-3893, www.sigersonmorrison.com; hours: M–Sa 11AM–7PM, Su 12PM–6PM)* for an elegantly retro pair of shoes.

LOWER EAST SIDE

Ⓕ *to Delancey St. or Second Ave.;*
ⒿⓏ *to Essex St.*

● **SNAPSHOT** ●

In the early years of the 20th century, the Lower East Side was the most densely populated area in the world. Primarily a Jewish neighborhood, its tenements were also crammed with immigrants from Eastern Europe, Italy, Germany, and Ireland, who worked in sweatshops and filled the streets with the neigh-borhood's distinctive pushcarts. Although the living conditions, as revealed by the muckraking journalist, Jacob A. Riis, in his book *How the Other Half Lives*, were often grim, the denizens of the Lower East Side gave back much to America. George Gershwin, Ira Gershwin, The Marx Brothers, Al Smith, and many others were born or grew up here. In the 1960s, the ethnic makeup of the Lower East Side began to change as the older immigrant groups moved out and Hispanics began to move in. Drawn by cheap rents, many artists, musicians, and writers joined the mélange.

PLACES TO SEE
Landmarks:

For anyone interested in history, the **Lower East Side Tenement Museum (39)** *(108 Orchard St., Broome/Delancey Sts., 212-982-8420, www.tenement. org; hours: daily first tour at 10:30AM, last tour at 5PM except for Thanksgiving, Christmas Day, and New Year's Day)* is a must. The exhibits in this old tenement building recapture the daily life of the families that once lived here. The museum can only be seen by guided tour, so book ahead—the tours are very popular. Many of the area's synagogues have now been converted into other uses or are in extreme disrepair, but the **Eldridge Street Synagogue (40)** *(12 Eldridge St., Canal/Division Sts., 212-219-0302, www.eldridgestreet. org; hours: open to the public Su–Th 10AM–5PM)*, the oldest, is still in use. Take note of its elaborate Moorish interiors.

Arts & Entertainment:

The Village Voice, *Time Out*, and *The New York Press* all provide listings for music around town. The specialty of **The Living Room (41)** *(154 Ludlow St., Rivington/ Stanton Sts., 212-533-7237, www.livingroomny.com)* is singer-songwriters; it's where Norah Jones got her start. For poetry readings, **ABC No Rio (42)** *(156 Rivington St., Clinton/Suffolk Sts., 212-254-3697, www.abcnorio.org)* offers "Our Unorganicized Reading" open mike series every Sunday afternoon. And after all this, if you're in the mood for a movie, the **Landmark's Sunshine Cinema (43)** *(143 E. Houston St., First/Second Aves., 212-330-8182,* *www.landmarktheatres.com)*, housed in what once was a Yiddish vaudeville theater, offers the kinds of independent art films you'd never find locally.

Kids:

The Lower East Side is a dense urban neighborhood full of fascinating history and other adult attractions. If your children are somewhat adventurous eaters they'll probably love **Katz's Delicatessen (44) ($)** *(205 E. Houston St. at Ludlow St., 212-254-2246, www.katzdeli.com; hours: Su 8AM–10:45PM, M–Tu 8AM–9:45PM, W–Th 8AM–10:45PM, F–Sa 8AM–2:45AM)*, **Yonah Schimmel's (56)** *(137 E. Houston St., Forsyth/Eldridge Sts., 212-477-2858, www.knishery.com; hours: Su–Th 9AM–7:30PM, F–Sa 9AM to 10:30PM)*, and **Kossar's Bialys (55)** *(367 Grand St., Essex/Norfolk Sts., 877-424-4597, www.kossarsbialys.com; hours: Su–Th 6AM–8PM, F 6AM–2PM, Su 6AM–8PM)*. For slightly older children, seven and up, the **Tenement Museum (39)** *(see "Landmarks," page 52)* may also prove of interest. The best playgrounds in the vicinity can be found in the East Village *(see East Village "Kids" section, page 61)*, though you'll come across numerous **community gardens** as you stroll around the Lower East Side—most of which are usually pretty child-friendly.

PLACES TO EAT & DRINK
Where to Eat:
Katz's Delicatessen (44) ($) *(205 E. Houston St. at Ludlow St., 212-254-2246, www.katzdeli.com; hours: Su 8AM–10:45PM, M–Tu 8AM–9:45PM, W–Th 8AM–10:45PM, F–Sa 8AM–2:45AM)*—grab a hot dog or a pastrami sandwich at this New York institution. **Bereket (45) ($)** *(187 E. Houston St. at Orchard St., 212-475-7700; hours: daily 24 hours)* is a 24-hour joint to watch the hipsters devour inexpensive Turkish fast food. The **Dumpling House (46) ($)** *(118 Eldridge St., Grand/Broome Sts., 212-625-8008, cash only; hours: daily 7:30AM–9:30PM)* is a little hole in the wall that serves delicious dumplings. A cozy Cambodian spot, **Kampuchea (47) ($)** *(78 Rivington St. at Allen St., 212-529-3901, www.kampucheanyc.com; hours: Tu–Th 5:30PM–11PM, F–Sa 5:30PM–12AM, Su 5PM–11PM)* opened to rave reviews. The hip and trendy have been gathering at **The Orchard (48) ($$$)** *(162 Orchard St., Stanton/Rivington Sts., 212-353-3570, www.theorchardny.com; hours: Tu–Sa 6PM–11PM)*, an American-Italian restaurant with must-have flatbreads.

Bars & Nightlife:
Happy Ending (49) *(302 Broome St., Forsyth/Eldridge Sts., 212-334-9676, www.happyendinglounge.com; hours: Tu 10PM–4AM, W–Sa 7PM–4AM)* offers cozy booths and, for the literati, the Happy Endings Reading Series on the fourth Wednesday of every month. **Max Fish (50)** *(178 Ludlow St., Houston/Stanton Sts., 212-529-3959, www.maxfish.com; hours: daily 5:30PM–4AM)* has been going for longer than most of the trendsetters who pack it

every night can remember. It's a curious place with a sense of décor that has to be seen to be believed, and has one of the most quintessential jukeboxes in the city, if you can hear it above the roar of the crowd. **'inoteca (51)** *(98 Rivington St. at Ludlow St., 212-614-0473, www.inotecanyc.com; hours: daily 12PM–3AM)* is a stylish place of brick walls and clean lines that serves an astounding number (more than 350) of wines by the glass and bottle, with excel-

lent bruschetta, cheeses, and other Italian delights. The staff is very knowledge-able, and even when the place is packed they'll take the time to answer your wine questions politely. **The Slipper Room (52)** *(167 Orchard St. at Stanton St., 212-253-7246, www.slipper room.com; hours: Su–Th 8PM–2AM, F–Sa 8PM–4AM)* is a long red room with booths on one side, a bar at the other, and a stage at the far end where patrons are treated to burlesque shows on weekends. It's quite expensive, but well worth the visit.

WHERE TO SHOP

Shopping in the Lower East Side is a rich cultural experience. The vendors on Orchard Street (53) may now speak Spanish instead of Yiddish, but they offer great bargains in clothing, shoes, and luggage. And if you're hungry, there's Russ & Daughters (54) *(179 East Houston St., Allen/Orchard Sts., 212-475-4880, www.russand daughters.com; hours: M–F 8AM–8PM, Sa 9AM–7PM,*

Su 8AM–5:30PM) for lox and other smoked fish, **Kossar's Bialys (55)** *(367 Grand St., Essex/Norfolk Sts., 877-424-4597, www.kossarsbialys.com; hours: Su–Th 6AM–8PM, F 6AM–2PM, Su 6AM–8PM)* for fresh-baked bialys and bagels, and don't miss **Yonah Schimmel's (56)** *(137 E. Houston St., Forsyth/Eldridge Sts., 212-477-2858, www.knishery.com; hours: Su–Th 9AM–7:30PM, F–Sa 9AM to 10:30PM)* for a hot knish. If you want to get that oh-so-cool lower east side dress, head to **Honey in the Rough (57)** *(161 Rivington St., Suffolk/Clinton Sts., 212-228-6415, www.honeyintherough.com; hours: M–Sa 12PM–8PM, Su 12PM–7PM)*. Of course, fashion comes with a hefty price tag.

WHERE TO STAY

A hotel in the Lower East Side? Years ago the idea would have seemed absurd. But it's a sign of the times that the luxurious **Hotel on Rivington (58)** **($$$$)** *(107 Rivington St., Essex/Ludlow Sts., 212-475-2600, www.hotelonrivington.com)* not only exists, but is

also an ultra-ritzy glass-enveloped 20-story tower complete with every amenity you can think of. A beacon of cool. Also on Rivington, but a lot less splashy, is **Off Soho Suites Hotel (59) ($-$$$)** *(11 Rivington St., Bowery/Chrystie St., 800-633-7646, www.offsoho.com)*, a strangely corporate name for what is a basic, good-value, no-nonsense place to stay.

EAST VILLAGE

6 *to Astor Place;* **N R** *to 8th St.-NYU;*
B D F M *to Broadway-Lafayette St.*

• SNAPSHOT •

The East Village tends to blur, in many people's minds, with the Lower East Side—they're both grungy, hip, and full of old tenement buildings—and in a way it's true. But there are differences between the two neighborhoods, and for the purposes of this guide the East Village is considered to begin north of Houston Street, and the Lower East Side south of it. Both the East Village and the Lower East Side have taken on new, post-immigrant lives as hotbeds for the arts in the years since WWII. They became the places where artists, musicians, and writers congregated after Greenwich Village began its inexorable climb to bourgeois respectability and astronomical real estate prices. The Beat generation found succor here in the '50s and '60s; later, Punk Rock was nurtured at the infamous CBGB's club on the Bowery, and artists such as Keith Haring and Jeff Koons turned the East Village into the nation's hippest artistic center. Then in the '70s heroin hit the neighborhood badly. In the '80s real estate developers began to see promise in the area and the term "East Village" became a relatively new and distinct appellation for the neighborhood. The old East Village did not go quietly into the night—there were riots in 1988 and 1995 as large numbers of squatters were evicted from its streets and parks, but its face inevitably began to change into what it is today, still an exciting, astonishingly multi-cultural human bazaar, but one with coffee shops (yes, Starbucks), delis, restaurants, and boutiques on every corner. Changed though it is, it remains one of the most vital parts of the city, and a stroll down its highly charged streets is mandatory for any pedestrian explorer of Manhattan.

PLACES TO SEE
Landmarks:

In the early 19th century the East Village was a wealthy middle-class neighborhood full of grand houses before the great waves of immigrants arrived in the late 19th century, followed in the 1950s by the raffish artists and other free spirits who turned it into New York's great Bohemia. Vestiges of this grand past can still be found amid the often-dreary tenement buildings, such as the **Nicholas and Elizabeth Stuyvesant Fish House (60)** *(21 Stuyvesant St., E. Ninth/E. 10th Sts.)*. Built in the Federal style in 1803 for the great-grandson of the last Dutch general of what was then New Amsterdam, it's one of the earliest residential buildings in the city. Its generous proportions and handsome brick façade make a stark contrast with the cramped dwellings that subsequent residents of the neighborhood usually endured. It's now owned by nearby Cooper Union and is the official residence of its president. As well as tenement buildings, the East Village has a number of lovely brick and brownstone row houses dating from the mid-19th century. For a particularly fine example, check out **151 Avenue B (61)** *(E. Ninth/E. 10th Sts.)*, also known as "Bird's House," as its ground floor was home to saxophonist Charlie Parker from 1950 to 1954. The **New York City Marble Cemetery (62)** *(52-74 E. Second St., First/Second Aves., 212-228-6401, www.nycmc.org; entrance may be arranged by special appointment)* is another survivor of the neighborhood's solid past. Unless you gain entry on one of the occasional public tours, you can only get a tantalizing peek through the gate at this charming cemetery where some of New York's most illustrious citizens are buried, including the original inhabitant of the Stuyvesant Fish House. **Grace Church (63)** *(802 Broadway at E. 10th St., 212-254-2000, www.gracechurchnyc.org)* is one of the most beautiful churches in the city—a delicate Gothic Revival creation with a particularly lovely steeple, and surrounding gardens. It's open to the public and offers concerts. The East Village's main public space is **Tompkins Square Park (64)** *(E. Seventh to E. 10th Sts., Aves. A/B)*. Like so many other parks in the city, this one has seen a major and controversial overhaul in recent years that resulted in the eviction of a large number of homeless people and subsequent radical re-landscaping to avoid those hidden pockets where insalubrious elements might dwell. With the rampant gentrification of recent years it's now a safe and family-friendly environment, though this being the East Village, the cross-section of residents who hang out here is still pretty eyebrow-raising.

Arts & Entertainment:

Legend has it that there are denizens of the East Village who never go above 14th Street. Their feeling is: why bother? If they want history, they can always go to **Cooper Union (65)** *(30 Cooper Square, E. Eighth St./ Fourth Ave., 212-353-4100, www.cooper.edu)*, New York's first free nonsectarian college, where Abraham Lincoln gave his famous "Right makes might" speech. If they want drama, **La MaMa E.T.C. (66)** *(74A E. Fourth St., Bowery/Second Ave., 212-475-7710, www.lamama.org)* offers edgier alternatives to Broadway. They specifically try to support and nourish artists of all nations and cultures. If literature is their love, the poetry readings at **St. Mark's-in-the-Bowery Church (67)** *(131 E. 10th St. at Second Ave., 212-674-0910)*, the **Bowery Poetry Club (68)** *(308 Bowery, Bleecker/Houston Sts., 212-614-0505, www.bowerypoetry.com)*, **KGB (69)** *(85 E. Fourth St., Second/Third Aves., 212-505-3360, www.kgbbar.com)* and the **Nuyorican Poets Café (70)** *(236 E. Third St., Aves. B/C, 212-505-8183, www.nuyorican.org)* beckon. The **Theater for the New City (71)** *(155 First Avenue, 9th/10th Sts., 212-254-1109, www.theaterforthenewcity.net)* produces 30-40 new American plays per year, of which about ten are by emerging, young playwrights. But that barely scratches the surface of all the East Village has to offer. It has the liveliest street life in the city. Walk down **St. Mark's Place (72)** to see a myriad of eccentric New Yorkers from art students, slackers, hipsters, to rock musicians, and revolutionaries. You may be inspired to get some ink, or a piercing, in one of the tattoo parlors that line the street. There's a thriving art scene with small galleries dotting the area. Check out **GRNY (73)** *(437 E. 9th St., 1st Ave/Ave A., 212-674-4769, www.grny.net; hours: M–Sa 11:30AM–8PM, Su 12PM–7PM)*, an offshoot gallery of *Giant Robot Magazine*, that specializes in Asian American pop culture. Or for emerging photographers, painters, and mixed-media artists visit the

Michael Mut Gallery (74) *(97 Avenue C, 6th/7th Sts., 212-677-7868, www.michaelmutgallery.com; hours: Th–Sa 1PM–6PM, Su 1PM–5PM).*

Kids:

The **First Street Playground (75)** *(Houston and E. First St., First/Second Aves.)* has plenty of shade and inventive climbing frames for younger children. **Tompkins Square Park (64)** *(E. Seventh to E. 10th Sts., Aves. A/B)* has no less than three separate and excellent playgrounds, complete with climbing frames, and all are safely enclosed from the street. There are also numerous highly funky and original children's stores around here. One of the best is Dinosaur Hill (76) *(306 E. Ninth St., First/Second Aves., 212-473-5850, www.dinosaurhill.com; hours: daily 11AM–7PM)*, which has a wonderful selection of wooden toys, puppets, wind-up toys, and other classics.

PLACES TO EAT & DRINK
Where to Eat:

Italian, Indian, Eastern European, Korean, Latin American, Mexican, even American—if you're looking for a great bargain meal, the East Village is the place to go. No matter what cuisine or ambience you're in the mood for, the East Village will probably have a restaurant to suit both your cravings and your pocket. On a cold winter's day, order a piping hot bowl of borscht at **Veselka (77) ($)** *(144 Second Ave. at E. Ninth St., 212-228-9682, www.veselka.com; hours: daily 24 hours)*, a gussied-up Ukrainian 24-hour-coffee shop (dig those crazy murals of East Village types on the walls). Hipsters, college students, and families crowd into

Two Boots Pizzeria (78) ($) *(42 Ave. A at 3rd St., 212-254-1919, www.twoboots.com: Su–Tu 11:30AM–11PM, W–Th 11:30AM–12AM, F–Sa 11:30AM–2AM)* for its pizzas and funky vibe. East Sixth Street between Second and First avenues (and now extending a tad eastward to Ave. A) is known as **Little India (79)**. **Brick Lane Curry House (80) ($-$$)** *(306-308 E. 6th St. at 2nd Ave., 212-979-8787, www.bricklanecurryhouse.com: Su–Th 1PM–11PM, F–Sa 1PM–1AM)* is a British-style curry shop known for spicy dishes. Come early if you don't want to wait in line at **Frank (81) ($)** *(88 Second Ave., E. Fifth/E. Sixth Sts., 212-420-0202, www.frankrestaurant. com; hours: Su 10:30AM–12AM, M–Th 10:30AM–1AM, F–Sa 10:30AM–2AM)*, a lively, homey restaurant that serves up heaping plates of Italian favorites. Delicious organic, vegan, world-fusion cuisine awaits you at **Caravan of Dreams (82) ($$)** *(405 E. 6th St., 1st Ave/Ave A, 212-254-1613, www.caravanofdreams.net; hours: Su–F 11AM–11PM, Sa 11AM–12AM)*. There's live music most every night. Young hipsters love **Dok Suni's (83) ($$)** *(119 First Ave., E. Seventh St./St. Marks Pl., 212-477-9506; hours: Su 12PM–11PM, M 4:30PM–11PM, Tu–F 4:30PM–12AM, Sa 12PM–12AM)* for its dark, dive bar décor and its garlicky Korean barbecue. If you have a yen for Japanese food, **Soba-ya (84) ($$)** *(229 E. 9th St., Second/Third Aves., 212-533-6966, www.sobaya-nyc.com; hours: lunch 12PM–3:30PM, dinner Su–Th 5:30PM–10:30PM F–Sa to 11PM)* serves up satisfying bowls of the noodles known as udon and a wide selection of Japanese beer. And if all this foreign food leaves you with a craving for Americana, get some fresh seafood at the **Mermaid Inn (85) ($$)** *(96 Second Ave., E. Fifth/E. Sixth Sts., 212-674-5870, www.themermaid nyc.com; hours: M 5:30PM–10PM, Tu–Th 5:30PM–11PM, F–Sa 5:30PM–11:30PM, Su 5PM–10PM).* Its wood-lined walls and casual décor evoke a New England fishing shack.

Bars & Nightlife:

The East Village has a hopping bar scene. Have a beer at the fabled **McSorley's Old Ale House (86)** *(15 E. Seventh St., Second/Third Aves., 212-473-9148, www.mcsorleys newyork.com; hours: M–Sa 11AM–1AM, Su 1PM–1AM).* Opened in 1854, this little piece of old New York has sawdust on the floors, old newspaper clippings on the wall, and its own ale. **Zum Schneider (87)** *(107 Ave. C at E. Seventh St., 212-598-1098, www.zumschneider.com; hours: M–Th opens at 5PM, F at 4PM, Sa–Sun at 1PM)* is a great place for German beer, with 12 kinds on tap. **Lakeside Lounge (88)** *(162 Ave. B, E. 10th/E. 11th Sts., 212-529-8463, www.lakeslounge.com; hours: daily 4PM–4AM)* is where you can hear lively rock bands without paying either a minimum or a cover. And if you're in the mood for something more sophisticated, walk up the stairs of **8 Stuyvesant St.** *(St. Marks Pl./E. Ninth St.)* and through the **Village Yokocho** Japanese restaurant into the tiny **Angel's Share (89)** *(212-777-5415; hours: Su–Th 6PM–1:30AM, F–Sa 6PM–2:30AM).* Collapse into one of the cozy armchairs and order a dry martini. Your Japanese waiter will mix it for you at your table. Enjoy it while gazing out the windows at Astor Place and the crowds below.

WHERE TO SHOP

The raffish **St. Mark's Place (72)** *(Eighth St., Third Ave./Ave. A)* is a jumble of CD stores, head shops, comic book shops, T-shirt and cheap jewelry stands, cafes and bars, and is crowded day and night. East of First Avenue, **Avenues A** and **B** have an artier, edgier vibe. **East Seventh Street** and **Stuyvesant Street** (a one-block gem between St. Mark's Place on Third Avenue and East Ninth Street) are beautiful tree-shaded, brownstone-lined streets where many off-beat clothing and jewelry designers have set up shop. If it's all too much for you, take time for a shvitz (Yiddish for steam bath) at the Russian Turkish Baths (90) *(268 E. 10th St., First Ave./Ave. A, 212-674-9250, www.russianturkish baths.com; hours: M coed 12PM–10PM; T coed 12PM–10PM; W women only 10AM–2PM, coed 2PM–10PM; Th men only 12PM–5PM, coed 5PM–10PM; F coed 12PM–10PM; Sa coed 9AM–10PM; Su men only 8AM–2PM, coed 2PM–10PM, shorts must be worn during coed hours)*. It's a perfect way to take a time-trip back to the days when the streets were packed with immigrants, Second Avenue was the Broadway of the Yiddish theater scene, and tenement apartments had a bathtub in the kitchen. If you're in the mood for something really different, pay the Russian masseuse to beat you with an oak branch—it's supposed to improve the circulation. Or join lines to get a cheap (and very memorable) haircut at Astor Place Hair (91) *(2 Astor Pl. at Broadway, 212-475-9854, www.astorplacehairnyc.com; hours: Su 9AM–6PM, M 8AM–8PM, Tu–F 8AM–10:30PM, Sa 8AM–8PM)*. Browsing (and even buying) is a major East Village sport. For books, try St. Mark's Bookshop (92) *(31 Third Ave., at E. Ninth St., 212-260-7853, www.stmarks bookshop.com; hours: M–Sa 10AM–12AM, Su 11AM–12AM)* for photography books, literary journals, and tons of trendy literati ambience. Kiehl's (93) *(109 Third Ave., E.13th/E.14th Sts., 212-677-3171, www. kiehls.com; hours: M–Sa 10AM–8PM, Su 11AM–6PM)*, a family-run pharmacy since the 19th century, now imports its distinctive lotions and shampoos, but the high-ceilinged emporium is still the place to go to be served by pleasant, knowledgeable salespeople in their pristine lab coats. St. Mark's Sounds (94) *(20 St. Mark's Pl., Second/Third Aves., 212-677-3444; hours: Su, W–Th 12PM–8PM, F–Sa 12PM–9PM, closed M–Tu, not always open at noon sharp)* is a great place for hard-to-find vintage vinyl. You can browse among the didgeri-doos (Australian Aboriginal musical instruments) at the one-of-a-kind music shop, Tribal Soundz (95) *(340 E. Sixth St., First/Second Aves., 212-673-5992, www. tribalsoundz.com; hours: daily 3PM until late)*. St. Mark's Place between Second and Third avenues is the place for punk gear; First Avenue and Avenue A are good for vintage clothing.

WHERE TO STAY

The East Village Bed & Coffee (96) (\$-\$\$) *(110 Ave. C, E. Seventh/E. Eighth Sts., 917-816-0071, www.bedand coffee.com)* is a walk-up brownstone with chic rooms, a private garden for guests, plus live-in hostess and her dog. A real New York gem.

chapter 3

NoHo
SoHo
Greenwich Village
Union Square

Places to See:

Places to Eat & Drink:

9. Two Boots To Go-Go
10. Noho Star
11. Great Jones Café
12. Five Points
13. BONDST
14. Tom and Jerry's
15. B Bar and Grill
16. Joe's Pub
29. Pepe Rosso To Go
30. Fanelli Cafe
31. Boqueria
32. Balthazar
33. Blue Ribbon Sushi
34. Ear Inn
35. Broome Street Bar
36. The Room
37. MercBar
38. Bar 89
39. Performing Garage
40. Don Hill's
41. S.O.B.'s
58. Caffé Reggio
59. Joe
60. Caffe Dante
77. Magnolia Bakery
78. Grey Dog Coffee
79. John's of Bleecker Street Pizzeria
80. Moustache
81. Tea & Sympathy
82. Pastis
83. Babbo
84. Lupa
85. Jane
86. White Horse Tavern
87. Hogs and Heifers
88. APT
89. The Otheroom
90. Monster
91. Village Vanguard
92. Blue Note
93. 55 Bar
94. The Bitter End
95. Zinc Bar
119. Chat 'n' Chew
120. 15 East
121. Rainbow Falafel and Shawarma
122. Union Square Café
123. Blue Water Grill
124. Japonais
125. Old Town Bar & Grill
126. Pete's Tavern
127. Heartland Brewery
128. Underbar
129. Irving Plaza

NOHO

Ⓑ Ⓓ Ⓕ Ⓜ *to Broadway-Lafayette St.;*
Ⓖ *to Bleecker St.*

● SNAPSHOT ●

In the 1970s, this area of warehouses north of Houston Street (hence its acronym NoHo for "North of Houston Street") began to draw artists escaping from the escalating rents of neighboring Soho. In 1976, the neighborhood was rezoned so that artists could both live and work there. Today, Noho is a small, but bustling, neighborhood known as much for its popular restaurants and cabaret as for its arts scene.

PLACES TO SEE
Landmarks:

Dating from only 2000, the **Noho Historic District** *(roughly E. Houston St. to Astor Pl., Broadway/Bowery)* is a fairly recent Landmarks designation, but it contains some astonishing buildings in a remarkable variety of styles and materials. The **Bayard-Condict Building (1)** *(65-69 Bleecker St., Broadway/Lafayette St.)* is an early skyscraper (13 stories!) and the only Louis Sullivan building in New York. Its lovely white terracotta façade has beautifully organic, ornate details. The **Bond Street Savings Bank (2)** *(330 Bowery, Bond/Great Jones Sts., now the Bouwerie Lane Theater)* is a handsome cast iron building in a robust French Baroque style that's now home to the Jean Cocteau Repertory Company. One of the finest of all New York's fire stations is the Beaux Arts **Fire Engine Company No. 33 (3)** *(44 Great Jones St., Lafayette St./Bowery)*. And in a different style altogether, go see the vast Romanesque bulk of the **DeVinne Press Building (4)** *(393-399 Lafayette St. at E. Fourth St.)*, which once housed famous publications such as *Scribner's Monthly* and *Century Illustrated Monthly Magazine*.

Arts & Entertainment:

The **Merchant's House Museum (5)** *(29 E. Fourth St., Lafayette St./Bowery, 212-777-1089, www.merchants house.com; hours: M, Th-Su 12PM–5PM)* is like a little trip back to the 19th century. This delightful Federal house is decorated with the original furniture of the wealthy family that lived there for several generations, and offers exhibitions and tours that reveal early 19th-century domestic life. Another remnant of the elegant lives of this period's successful citizens can be found in the four remaining town houses of what was once called **Colonnade Row (6)** *(428-434 Lafayette St., Astor Pl./Great Jones St.)*. Check out the plays at the **Public Theater (7)** *(425 Lafayette St., Astor Pl./E. Fourth St., 212-539-8500, www.publictheater.org)*. If you're into the gallery scene, check out **Zürcher Studio (8)** *(33 Bleecker St., at Mott St., 212-777-0790, www.galeriezurcher.com; hours: Tu–Sa 12PM–6PM, Su 2PM–6PM)* for painting, photography, video, sculpture, and installations by emerging artists from France and abroad.

PLACES TO EAT & DRINK
Where to Eat:

For great pizza at a great price, **Two Boots To Go-Go (9) ($)** *(74 Bleecker St. at Broadway, 212-777-1033, www.two boots.com; hours: M–Th 11AM–12AM, F–Sa 11AM–1AM, Su 11AM–11PM)* is both kid and adult friendly. The **Noho Star (10) ($$)** *(330 Lafayette St. at Bleecker St., 212-925-0070, www.nohostar.com; hours: M–F 8AM–12AM, Sa 10:30AM–12AM, Su 10:30AM–11PM)* dishes up good burgers and other American food, and the lively **Great Jones Café (11) ($$)** *(54 Great Jones St., Bowery/ Lafayette Sts., 212-674-9304, www.greatjones.com; hours: Tu–F 12PM–4PM, M–Th 5PM–12AM, Fri–Sa 5PM–1AM, week-end brunch 11:30AM–4PM)* has tasty Cajun cuisine. For a glimpse of more fashionable people at play, **Five Points (12) ($$)** *(31 Great Jones St., Bowery/Lafayette St., 212-253-5700, www.fivepointsrestaurant.com; hours: lunch M–F 12PM–3PM; dinner M–F 5:30PM–11PM, Sa 5:30PM–11:30PM, Su 5:30PM–10PM; brunch Sa–Su 11AM–3PM)* features creative American cuisine, and **BONDST (13) ($$$)** *(6 Bond St., Broadway/Lafayette St., 212-777-2500, www.bondstrestaurant.com; hours: Su–M 6PM–11PM, Tu–Sa 6PM–12AM)* is known for its sushi.

Bars & Nightlife:

Bar 288, also known as **Tom and Jerry's (14)** *(288 Elizabeth St., Bleecker/Houston Sts., 212-260-5045; hours: daily 12PM–4AM)*, has a wide selection of beers. And if you're in the mood to see and be seen go to the former gas station now known as **B Bar and Grill (15)** *(40 E. Fourth St., Bowery/Lafayette St., 212-475-2220, www.bbarandgrill.com; hours: M, W 11AM–1AM, Tu, F 11AM–4AM, Th 11AM–2AM, Sa 10AM–4AM, Su 10AM–1AM)*. **Joe's Pub (16)** *(425 Lafayette St., Astor Place/ E. Fourth St., 212-539-8778, www.joespub.com; hours: dinner daily 6PM–12:30AM)*, located in the **Public Theater (7)**, is one of the most innovative and popular places to go for cabaret in the city.

WHERE TO SHOP

Along with art supplies, Blick Art Materials (17) *(1-5 Bond St., Broadway/Lafayette St., 212-533-2444, www.dickblick.com; hours: M–F 9AM–8PM, Sa 10AM– 7PM, Su 11AM–6PM)* sells journals, stationery, and art books. If you're in the market for unique souvenirs, Bond No. 9 New York (18) *(9 Bond St., Broadway/ Lafayette St., 212-228-1732, www.bondno9.com; hours: M–F 11AM–8PM, Sa 10AM–7PM, Su 12PM–6PM)* sells elegant perfumes named after different New York City neighborhoods. For CDs and DVDs, head to Other Music (19) *(15 E. 4th St., Broadway/Lafayette, 212-477-8150, www.othermusic.com; hours: M–F 12PM–9PM, Sa 12PM–8PM, Su 12PM–7PM)*, an indie-music mecca, which carries artists not found elsewhere and hosts in-store performances.

N **R** *to Prince St.;* **C** **E** *to Spring St.;*
6 *to Spring St.;* **B** **D** **F** **M** *to Broadway-Lafayette St.*

● SNAPSHOT ●

The neighborhood now known as Soho has gone through many lives. In the years after the Civil War, its distinctive cast-iron warehouses housed many textile companies and other light manufacturers. By the mid-20th century, however, many of the manufacturers had moved on. Drawn by Soho's cobblestone streets, cheap rents, and huge loft spaces, many artists then made the neighborhood their own. In 1972, Soho was rezoned as a residential neighborhood as well as a manufacturing one, and the next year it was designated the SoHo Cast Iron Historic District. Rents began to soar. Today, it is the rare artist who can afford a Soho loft. The once half-empty streets of Soho are now packed with locals and tourists who come for the upscale trendy shopping and the galleries and museums.

PLACES TO SEE
Landmarks:

In the 19th century, cast iron was a popular building material. Strong and easily molded, a cast-iron façade could add elegance and durability to a plain brick building. Soho has the largest collection of cast-iron buildings in the world. Both solid-looking and fanciful, these early precursors to the skyscraper give Soho a cinematic ambience. Some of the more famous buildings are the **Singer Building (20)** *(561-563 Broadway, Prince/Spring Sts.)* and the **E. V. Haughwout & Co. Store (21)** *(488-492 Broadway, Spring/Broome Sts.)*.

Arts & Entertainment:

The **Angelika Film Center (22)** *(18 W. Houston St. at Mercer St., 212-995-2000, www.angelikafilm center.com)* shows independent and art films. Come early to enjoy refreshments beneath a huge chandelier at the theater cafe. **The Drawing Center (23)** *(35 Wooster St., Broome/Grand Sts., 212-219-2166, www.drawingcenter.org; hours: W, F–Sa 12PM–6PM, Th 12PM–8PM)* is a nonprofit gallery dedicated to promoting the art and appreciation of drawing. **Artists Space (24)** *(38 Greene St., Broome/Grand Sts., 3rd fl., 212-226-3970, www.artistsspace.org; hours: Tu–Sa 12PM–6PM during exhibitions only)* is another non-profit gallery that gives group shows focused on a theme. Many artists have gotten their start here. Among private galleries, **Deitch Projects (25)** *(76 Grand St., Wooster/Greene Sts., 212-343-7300, www.deitch.com; hours: Tu–Sa 12PM–6PM)*, and **Janet Borden Gallery (26)** *(560 Broadway, Prince/Spring Sts., 212-431-0166, www.janetbordeninc.com; hours: Tu–Sa 11AM–5PM)* are some of the most interesting. **Animazing Gallery (27)** *(54 Greene St., at Broome St., 212-226-7374, www.animazing.com; hours: M–Sa 10AM–7PM, Su 11AM–6PM)* includes illustration art by Maurice Sendak, Tim Burton, and other notable artists.

Kids:

The **New York City Fire Museum (28)** *(278 Spring St., Hudson/Varick Sts., 212-691-1303, www.nycfiremuseum. org; hours: Tu–Sa 10AM–5PM, Su 10AM–4PM)* is a 1904 firehouse that has a collection of old fire engines and equipment as well as displays dedicated to the history of firefighting, including the sad, heroic time during and after September 11, 2001.

PLACES TO EAT & DRINK
Where to Eat:

Pepe Rosso To Go (29) ($) *(149 Sullivan St., W. Houston/Prince Sts., 212-677-4555, www.peperossotogo. com; hours: daily 11AM–11PM)* started as an Italian take-out joint, but has added a few tables. Good pasta, great prices. When Soho was still a nameless artists' and factory neighborhood, **Fanelli Cafe (30) ($$)** *(94 Prince St. at Mercer St., 212-226-9412; hours: Su–Th 10AM–1:30AM, F–Sa 10AM–3AM)*, a 19th-century bar, was practically the only watering hole. It still has a raffish, artistic air. Come for a beer, the good bar food, and a glimpse of what things used to be like not so long ago. If you like tapas, try **Boqueria (31) ($-$$)** *(171 Spring St., 212-343-4255, www.boquerianyc.com; hours: daily 12PM–12AM)*. This Soho spot reels in seafood lovers who enjoy small-plate dining. **Balthazar (32) ($$$)** *(80 Spring St., Broadway/Crosby St., 212-965-1414, www. balthazarny.com; hours: continental breakfast M–F 7:30AM–11:30AM, Sa–Su 8AM–10AM; brunch Sa–Su 10AM–4PM; lunch M–F 12PM–5PM; dinner M–Th 5:45PM–12AM, F–Sa 5:45PM–1AM, Su 5:30PM–12AM)* is

famous for its delicious French bistro
food, turn-of-the-century French décor,
and glamorous patrons. **Blue Ribbon
Sushi (33) ($$)** *(119 Sullivan St.,
Prince/Spring Sts., 212-343-0404, www.
blueribbonrestaurants.com: daily 12PM–*

2AM) is always crowded, though patrons say it's worth
the wait. A favorite of chefs, who will stop by to have a
bite after work.

Bars & Nightlife:

What would an artists' neighborhood be without an old,
dark, dive bar or two? Soho has a fair number. Besides
Fanelli Cafe (30) *(see page 76)*, there's the **Ear Inn (34)** *(326
Spring St., Greenwich/Washington Sts., 212-226-9060,
www.earinn.com; hours: daily 12PM–4AM)*, which claims
to be New York City's oldest bar, and the **Broome Street
Bar (35)** *(363 West Broadway at Broome St., 212-925-
2086, www.broomestreetbar.ypguides.net; hours: Su–Th
11AM–1:30AM, F–Sa 11AM–2:30AM)*. For a quiet, more
upscale evening, locals like **The Room (36)** *(144 Sullivan
St., Houston/Prince Sts., 212-477-2102, www.the
otheroom.com; hours: daily 5PM–4AM)* for a good selec-
tion of wines and beers in an intimate atmosphere. If
you want to pretend you're a rock star, **MercBar (37)** *(151
Mercer St., Houston/Prince Sts., 212-966-2727, www.
mercbar.com; hours: Su–Th 5PM–2AM, F–Sa 5PM–4AM)*
in the very hip Mercer Hotel, or **Bar 89 (38)** *(89 Mercer
St., Broome/Spring Sts., 212-274-0989, www.bar89.com;
hours: Su–Th 12PM–1AM, F–Sa 12PM–2AM)* will provide
the perfect settings. Spalding Gray got his start at the

Performing Garage (39) *(33 Wooster St., Broome/Grand Sts., 212-966-9796, www.thewoostergroup.org).* This alternative theater continues to be the home for a variety of innovative work. Downed too many beers at the **Ear Inn (34)**? Listen to soul and hip hop at **Don Hill's (40)** *(511 Greenwich St. at Spring St., 212-219-2850, www.donhills.com; call or look online for show times).* Dance the mambo or the merengue at **S.O.B.'s (41)** (Sounds of Brazil) *(204 Varick St., W. Houston/King Sts., 212-243-4940, www.sobs.com; call or look online for show times).* This venerable club features live music not only from Brazil, but from all over Latin America, the Mideast, Africa, and the Caribbean.

WHERE TO SHOP

If you're in the market for ultra-chic, artsy clothing, and money is burning a hole in your pocket, Soho is the place. Anna Sui (42) *(113 Greene St., Prince/Spring Sts., 212-941-8406, www.annasui.com; hours: M–Sa 11AM–7PM, Su 12PM–6PM),* Marc Jacobs (43) *(163 Mercer St., Houston/Prince Sts., 212-343-1490, www.marcjacobs.com; hours: M–Sa 11AM–7PM, Su 12PM–6PM),* Anthropologie (44) *(375 West Broadway, Spring/ Broome Sts., 212-343-7070, www.anthropologie.com; hours: M–Sa 11AM–8PM, Su 11AM–6PM),* and Prada (45) *(575 Broadway at Prince St., 212-334-8888, www.prada.com; hours: M–Sa 11AM–8PM, Su 12PM–7PM)* are just a few destinations. Add cooler-than-thou European shoes from Camper (46) *(125 Prince St. at Wooster St., 212-358-1842, www.camper.com; hours: M–Sa 11AM–8PM, Su 12PM–6PM).* Or try Kenneth Cole New York (47) *(595 Broadway, Houston/Prince Sts., 212-*

965-0283, www.kennethcole.com; hours: Su 11AM–7PM, M–W 10AM–8PM, Th–Sa 10AM–9PM). To polish your look, go for cosmetics from the Swedish company **FACE Stockholm (48)** *(110 Prince St. at Greene St., 212-966-9110, www.face stockholm.com; hours: M–Sa 11AM–7PM, Su 12PM–6PM)*. Underneath it all, some sexy lingerie from **Agent Provocateur (49)** *(133 Mercer St., Prince/Spring Sts., 212-965-0229, www.agentprovocateur.com; hours: M–Sa 11AM–7PM, Su 12PM–6PM)* is a per-fect choice. If you're on a tight budget, the

Chinese department store **Pearl River Mart (50)** *(477 Broadway, Broome/Grand Sts., 212-431-4770, www.pearl river.com; hours: daily 10AM–7:20PM)* sells gorgeous silk jackets, blouses, porcelain, teas, lighting, and souvenirs at bargain prices. And the collection of exquisite journals, stationery, and handmade papers at **Kate's Paperie (51)** *(72 Spring St. between Crosby and Lafayette Sts., 212-941-9816, www.katespaperie.com; hours: M–Sa 10AM–8PM, Su 11AM–7PM)* will make you want to write home.

WHERE TO STAY

If you want to see how the very beautiful people live, **The Mercer (52)** *($$$$) (147 Mercer St. at Prince St., 212-966-6060, www.mercerhotel.com)* has high-fashion interiors, marble bathrooms, a 24-hour concierge and room service, in a heart-of-Soho locale. The **Holiday Inn Downtown/Soho (53)** *($$-$$$) (138 Lafayette St., Canal/Howard Sts., 212-966-8898, www.holidayinn.com)* is pleasant, clean, convenient, and cheap.

A **C** **E** *to West Fourth St. or 14th St.;*
B **D** **F** **M** *to West Fourth St.;* **F** **M** *to 14th St.;*
1 **2** **3** *to 14th St.;* **1** *to Christopher St.*

● SNAPSHOT ●

"The Village," as it's known to New Yorkers, has long been a refuge. In the 17th and 18th centuries, it was a sleepy country town to which New Yorkers fled in order to escape various plagues. In the 19th century, Italian immigrants came, bringing their cafes, bakeries, churches, and pizzerias with them. These days, the crooked tree-lined streets of the Village have become prime celebrity-spotting territory, as many actors and models have made it their home. But more than anything, this neighborhood has always drawn those attracted by its air of tolerance. The list of writers, painters, actors, musicians, and revolutionaries who have lived or hung out in this neighborhood would fill an encyclopedia. Among them are Edgar Allan Poe, Mark Twain, Edna St. Vincent Millay, Richard Wright, Jack Kerouac, Edward Hopper, Cary Grant, John Barrymore, Bob Dylan, and

John Reed, and that's just for starters. The Village is also where many say the gay liberation movement was born— on June 28, 1969, to be exact, when a police raid on The Stonewall Inn, a gay bar at 51 Christopher Street, evolved into the Stonewall Riots. The

Stonewall Inn has moved to 53 Christopher Street, and the surrounding neighborhood, with its gay bars and clubs, is still considered a gay Mecca.

PLACES TO SEE
Landmarks:

There are two things to realize before you begin your tour of The Village. First, the Village was not built on a numbered grid system, the way most of Manhattan was, but grew organically out of a network of rural paths. The result is some crazy cartographical anomalies, such as the corner where West 12th Street crosses West Fourth. It's easy to get lost. But the Village is quite safe and very walkable, and as you turn down some surprising alleyway, you'll soon discover that getting lost is part of the fun. The other thing to keep in mind is that there are really two villages: Greenwich Village, whose central plaza is Washington Square Park, and the West Village, the area surrounding Sheridan Square.

A good place to start a Greenwich Village tour is at **Washington Square Park (54)**, at the base of Fifth Avenue. Once a potter's field and a site for public hangings, this park is a haven for guitar strummers, chess players, street performers, NYU students, and those reliving the area's beatnik past. Its most notable feature is the **Washington Square Arch** (*NE side of Washington Square*), designed by the architect Stanford White and erected in 1895 to commemorate George Washington's inauguration. Check out the elegant

Greek revival town houses on **Washington Square North**. When they were built in the 1830s, they were some of the most exclusive residences in town. Henry James's grandmother owned one. Now most of them are owned by **NYU**. Its campus is scattered in buildings all over Greenwich Village. You might also want to peek in at **Washington Mews (55)** *(Washington Square North and East Eighth St.)*. This quaint cobblestone street was once where the horses of the aristocracy were stabled and the servants lived. The **Brown Building (56)** *(23-29 Washington Place, at Greene St.)*, now home to classrooms and offices of **NYU**, was previously the **Triangle Shirtwaist Factory Building**—the site of a tragic fire in 1911 which claimed the lives of 146 workers, most of them young women. Two years earlier it had been the site of one of the first major strikes by women workers in the history of the United States. One of the union's major complaints was the need for fire safety. Those needs were ignored and two years later missing fire escapes and locked doors were to blame for one of the worst industrial disasters in America. It led to major labor reform. Although the building is closed to the public, there is a plaque commemorating the workers at the corner of the building.

The streets around Washington Square were popular in the 1950s, 1960s, and early 1970s with abstract expressionists, folkies, beatniks, and war resisters. Washington Square South turns into **West Fourth Street (57)**, the inspiration for Bob Dylan's "Positively Fourth Street." Sullivan, Thompson, Bleecker, and MacDougal streets were once places to catch a wild poetry reading, buy some handmade sandals or silver jewelry, and sip a cappuccino in the days long before there was a Starbucks on every corner. The handmade sandals, and the beatniks who wore them, are gone, but the old cafes remain, still pleasant places to while away an afternoon. Try **Caffé Reggio (58)** *(119 MacDougal St. at W. Third St., 212-475-9557, www.caffereggio.com; hours: M–Th 8AM–3AM, F–Sa 8AM–4:30AM, Su 9AM–3AM)*, **Joe (59)** *(141 Waverly Pl., Gay St./6th Ave., 212-924-6750, www.joethe artofcoffee.com; hours: M–Sa 7AM–8PM, Su 8AM–8PM)*, or **Caffe Dante (60)** *(79 MacDougal St., Bleecker/W. Houston Sts., 866-681-0299, www.caffe-dante.com; hours: Su–Th 10AM–2AM, F–Sa 10AM–3AM)*. For those interested in the history of rock, there's Jimi Hendrix's **Electric Lady Sound Studios (61)** *(52 W. Eighth St., Fifth/Sixth Aves., 212-677-4700, www.electricladystudios.com)*.

Along with the Washington Arch, Greenwich Village's most distinctive architectural landmark is the **Jefferson Market Library (62)** *(425 Sixth Ave., W. 9th/W. 10th Sts., 212-243-4334; hours: M, W 9AM–8PM; Tu, Th 10AM–6PM; F–Sa 10AM–5PM)*. This red brick castle with its fairy-tale watchtower was originally designed as a courthouse by the Central Park designer Calvert Vaux in 1876. Vacated in 1945, it stood empty for 20 years and was slated for demolition when the efforts of community organizers resulted in the current renovation. It was opened as a public library in 1967. There are some charming streets in this area. Among them are **Patchin Place (63)** *(off W. 10th St., Greenwich/Sixth Aves.)*, a quiet iron-gated mews containing a number of three-story houses (4 Patchin Place was the home of poet e. e. cummings). **West 11th Street** *(Fifth/Sixth Aves.)* and **West 12th Street** *(Fifth/ Sixth Aves.)* is where **The New School (64)** *(66 West 12th St., www.newschool.edu)*—founded by radical intellectuals in 1919—is located.

A walk west will take you toward Greenwich Village's other square, **Sheridan Square (65)** *(Commerce St./W. Fourth St./Seventh Ave.)*, though in true got-to-be-different Village style, it's actually more of a triangle. Nearby Bedford Street is known for two houses that stand next to each other: **77 Bedford (66)** *(Morton/Commerce Sts.)*—the Isaac-Hendricks House—the oldest house in the Village, built in 1799; and **75-1/2 Bedford (66)**, only 9-and-a-half-feet wide, once the home of Edna St. Vincent Millay and later John Barrymore. The **Church of St. Luke's in the Fields (67)** *(487 Hudson St., Grove/ Christopher Sts., 212-924-0562, www.stlukeinthefields.org; hours: open for prayer and meditation M–F 10AM–2PM, 5:45PM–7PM, Su 7:30AM–3PM or until 1PM in summer)*, built in 1822, is one of the lovelier churches in the city. And if you're getting tired of quaint, amble over to the glass towers of **Perry West (68)** *(176 Perry St., corner of West St.)*. This apartment complex, designed by the modernist architect Richard Meier and opened in 2003, has already become the home of such celebrities as Nicole Kidman and Calvin Klein.

Gentrification has transformed New York in the past 30 years. The **Meatpacking District (69)** is the latest neighborhood to have undergone the process. This four-block enclave of cobblestone streets near the waterfront was once the home of more than a dozen meat-processing plants. Some of the plants still remain, but they have to battle for space with bars, restaurants, and boutiques that sell exquisite little handbags and designer togs. The Meatpacking District is best seen at night, when the combination of old warehouses, old memories, and up-to-the-minute bistros (with clientele to match) creates a very urban glamor.

Arts & Entertainment:

The famous poet and Greenwich Village resident Edna St. Vincent Millay was the founder of the **Cherry Lane Theatre (70)** *(38 Commerce St., Seventh Ave./Bedford St., 212-989-2020, www.cherrylanetheatre.com)*. Begun in 1924, it was the first Off-Broadway theater, and still hosts experimental theater, mixing it with more mainstream productions. Its tiny space offers an intimate theatrical experience. The **Actors Playhouse (71)** *(100 Seventh Ave. South, Bleecker/Christopher Sts., 212-255-6452, www.nyactors playhouse.com)* is another famous Off-Broadway spot that garners widespread attention. If you like stand-up, the **Comedy Cellar (72)** *(117 MacDougal St., W. Third/Bleecker Sts., 212-254-3480, www.comedycellar.com; hours: two shows Su–Th 9PM,11PM; three shows F 8PM, 9:45PM, 11:30PM; four shows Sa 7:30PM, 9:15PM, 11PM, 12:45AM)* is one of the more prestigious places for comics, and big names such as Jerry Seinfeld and Ray

Romano make frequent appearances to brush up on their audience skills. Like bowling, but kind of prefer drinking and flirting more? The gleamingly retro **Bowlmor Lanes (73)** *(110 University Pl., 12th/13th Sts., 212-255-8188, www.bowlmor.com; hours: M 4PM–2AM, Tu 4PM–1AM, W 4PM–1AM, Th 4PM–2AM, F 11PM–3:30AM, Sa 11AM–3:30AM, Su 11AM–12AM)* is for you, and you may well spot some of Hollywood's younger stars disporting themselves inappropriately. The Village, for all its attractions, isn't a museum hot spot, but it is the site of one of the best, and certainly the quirkiest, small museums in New York, the **Forbes Magazine Galleries (74)** *(60 Fifth Ave. at W. 12th St., 212-206-5548, www.forbesgalleries.com, entrance is free; hours: Tu–Sa 10AM–4PM)*. The late gazillionaire Malcolm Forbes was a man who liked to have fun, and the gallery is a memorial to his passions, from toy boats to stray pieces of memorabilia, all arranged with wit and a touchingly personal sense. NYU offers its own exhibition space with the little-known but absolutely first-rate **Grey Art Gallery (75)** *(NYU Silver Center, 100 Washington Square East, corner of Washington Pl., 212-998-6780, www. nyu.edu/greyart; hours: Tu, Th, F 11AM–6PM, W 11AM–8PM, Sa 11AM–5PM)*, featuring a 6,000-piece permanent collection of late 19th-century to early 20th-century art, including works by Picasso, de Kooning, and Miró.

Kids:

It may scare younger or more sensitive kids, but the annual **Halloween Day Parade** *(www.halloween-nyc.com)* that snakes its way up Sixth Avenue every October is incredible fun. A mix of ghosts, goblins, superheroes, stilt-walkers, drag queens, and, inevitably, endless Elvis Presleys, all wow the good-natured

crowd. The **Carmine Street Playground (76)** *(32 Carmine St., Bleecker/Bedford Sts.)* is one of the best in the Village. Head through the narrow passageway into a delightful safe play area full of climbing frames and toys.

PLACES TO EAT & DRINK
Where to Eat:

Although the Village certainly has some expensive (and worth it) restaurants, a budget traveler can eat extremely well here. In fact, some of the Village's most popular restaurants are also among its most reasonable. For breakfast, the **Magnolia Bakery (77) ($)** *(401 Bleecker St. at W. 11th St., 212-462-2572, www.magnoliabakery.com; hours: Su–Th 9AM–11PM, F–Sa 9AM–12AM)* and **Grey Dog Coffee (78) ($)** *(33 Carmine St., Bedford/Bleecker Sts., 212-462-0041, www.thegreydog.com; hours: M–Th 6:30AM–11:30PM, F 6:30AM–12:30AM, Sa 7:30AM–12:30AM, Su 7:30AM–11:30PM)* are great places for coffee and baked goods. For New York pizza, **John's of Bleecker Street Pizzeria (79) ($)** *(278 Bleecker St., Sixth/Seventh Aves., 212-243-1680, www.johnsbrickovenpizza.com; hours: M–Th 11:30AM–11:30PM, F 11:30AM–12AM, Sa*

11:30AM–12:30AM, Su 12PM–11:30PM) has been serving customers brick oven pies since the 1920s. (The only

caveat: John's does not serve slices, so bring a big appetite or a group to share a pie.) For inexpensive Middle Eastern fare, try **Moustache (80) ($)** *(90 Bedford St., Barrow/ Grove Sts., 212-229-2220, www. moustachepitza.com; hours: daily 12PM–11PM).* On a rainy afternoon you might enjoy high tea at **Tea & Sympathy (81) ($$)** *(108 Greenwich Ave., W. 12th/W. 13th Sts., 212-989-9735, www.teaandsympathynewyork.com; hours: M–F 11:30AM–10:30PM, Sa–Su 9:30AM–10:30PM),* served in an eccentric English atmosphere. If you're in the mood for a blow out, try **Pastis (82) ($$)** *(9 Ninth Ave. at Little 12th St., 212-929-4844, www.pastisny.com; hours: M–W 8AM–11:15AM, 12PM–1AM; Th 8AM–11:15AM, 12PM–2AM, F 8AM–11:15AM, 12PM–2:30AM, Sa 10AM–4:15PM, 6PM–2:30AM Su 10AM–4:15PM, 6PM–1AM),* a raucous French bistro in the Meatpacking District, for oysters and a glimpse at the beautiful people. Italian food is always a good choice in the Village. Probably the most coveted table in town is at **Babbo (83) ($$$)** *(110 Waverly Pl., MacDougal St./Sixth Ave., 212-*

777-0303, www.babbonyc.com; hours: M–Sa 5:30PM–11:15PM, Su 5PM–10:45PM; wine bar open M–Sa 5PM, Su 4:30PM), owned by superstar chef and local character, Mario Batali. Those on a more moderate budget might try another one of Batali's restaurants,

Lupa (84) ($$) *(170 Thompson St., Bleecker/W. Houston St., 212-982-5089, www.luparestaurant.com; hours: daily 12PM–12AM).* Finally, if all this cosmopolitanism gives you a craving for good American food and moderate prices, **Jane (85) ($$)** *(100 W. Houston St., La Guardia Pl./Thompson St., 212-254-7000, www.janerestaurant. com; hours: M–Th 11:30AM–11PM, F 11:30AM–12AM, Sa 11AM–12AM, Su 10AM–10PM)* serves chops, seafood, and deliciously gooey desserts in an understated elegant setting.

Bars & Nightlife:

White Horse Tavern (86) *(567 Hudson St. at W. 11th St., 212-989-3956; hours: Su–Th 11AM–2AM, F–Sa 11AM–4AM),* is where poet Dylan Thomas went on his last drinking binge before dying a few hours later. The former biker bar, **Hogs and Heifers (87)** *(859 Washington St. at W. 13th St., 212-929-0655, www.hogsand heifers.com; hours: M–F 11AM–4AM, Sa 1PM–4AM, Su 2PM–4AM)* is not nearly as down-and-dirty as it once was, though the girl bartenders still dance on the countertops, and the walls are decorated with discarded bras. For quieter evenings, try the glamorous lounge **APT (88)** *(419 W. 13th St., Ninth Ave./Washington St., 212-414-4245, www.aptnyc.com; hours: nightly 7PM–4AM)* and the sophisticated **The Otheroom (89)** *(143 Perry St., Greenwich/Washington Sts., 212-645-9758, www.theotheroom.com; hours:*

Su–M 5PM–2AM, Tu–Sa 5PM–4AM). And if you're interested in the gay scene, the **Monster (90)** *(80 Grove St., Waverly Pl./W. Fourth St., 212-924-3558, www. manhattan-monster.com; hours: M–F 4PM–4AM, Sa–Su 2PM–4AM)* caters to men, as it has for a long time. The

Village is the home of some famous jazz clubs, such as the **Village Vanguard (91)** *(178 Seventh Ave. South, corner of W. 11th St., 212-255-4037, www. villagevanguard.com; hours: sets at 9PM and 11PM nightly, with an additional 12:30AM set on an occasional Sa)* and the **Blue Note (92)** *(131 W. Third St., MacDougal St./Sixth Ave., 212-475-8592, www.bluenotejazz.com; hours: shows Su–F at 8PM and 10:30PM, additional shows F, Sa 12:30AM)*. These famous clubs can be pricey, however. Some inexpensive (and very popular) clubs to try are the **55 Bar (93)** *(55 Christopher St., Sixth/Seventh Aves., 212-929-9883, www.55bar.com; daily music)* and **The Bitter End (94)** *(147 Bleecker St., Thompson St./La Guardia Pl., 212-673-7030, www.bitterend.com; check schedule for daily music)*, where legends like Bob Dylan and Billy Joel have played. **Zinc Bar (95)** *(90 W. Houston St. at La Guardia Pl., 212-477-8337, www.zincbar.com; hours: Su–Th 6PM–2:30AM, F–Sa 6PM–3AM)* has a variety of sounds featured, including Brazilian jazz, jazz vocals, and poetry readings.

WHERE TO SHOP

One of the first fashion designers to head to the Meatpacking District was **Jeffrey New York (96)** *(449 W.*

14th St., Ninth/10th Aves., *212-206-1272, www.jeffreynewyork.com; hours: M–W, F 10AM–8PM; Th 10AM–9PM; Sa 10AM–7PM; Su 12:30PM–6PM)*, whose simple yet stylish clothes attract models and actresses like moths to a flame. Somewhat more downmarket is **Urban Outfitters (97)** *(374 Sixth Ave. at Waverly Pl., 212-677-9350, www.urbanoutfitters.com; hours: M–Sa 10AM–9PM, Su 11AM–8PM)*, which sells hipster gear for those on a budget. For something sexy to wear beneath, **La Petite Coquette (98)** *(51 University Pl., W. Ninth/W. 10th Sts., 888-473-5799, www. thelittleflirt.com; hours: M–W 11AM–7PM, Th 11AM–8PM, F–Sa 11AM–7PM, Su 12PM– 6PM)* is a good choice for gorgeous lingerie.

New Yorkers looking for cheap fashionable shoes will browse the shoe stores on **East 8th Street (99)** *(Fifth/Sixth Aves.)*. **C. O. Bigelow (100)** has been standing at 414 Sixth Avenue *(W. Eighth/W. Ninth Sts., 212-533-2700, www.bigelowchemists.com; hours: M–F 7:30AM–9PM, Sa 8:30AM–7PM, Su 8:30AM–5PM)* for more than 150 years. It offers a quirky collection of American and European lotions and soaps. The streets around Bleecker and Sixth Avenue have many shops catering to the music lover. For rare records try **Bleecker Bob's Golden Oldies Record Shop (101)** *(118 W. Third St.,*

MacDougal St./Sixth Ave., 212-475-9677; hours: Su–Th 11AM–1AM, F–Sa 11AM–3AM) or **Bleecker Street Records (102)** *(239 Bleecker St., Carmine/Leroy Sts., 212-255-7899, www.bleeckerstreetrecords.com; hours: Su–Th 11AM–10PM, F–Sa 11AM–11PM).* **Matt Umanov Guitars (103)** *(273 Bleecker St., Sixth/Seventh Aves., 212-675-2157, www.umanovguitars.com; hours: M–Sa 11AM–7PM, Su 12PM–6PM)* has long been famous for its collection of both acoustic and electric instruments. One of the city's best independent bookstores is **Three Lives & Company (104)** *(154 W. 10th St. at Waverly Pl., 212-741-2069, www.threelives.com; hours: Su 12PM–7PM, M–Tu 12PM–8PM, W–Sa 11AM–8:30PM),* which has a knowledgeable staff and an excellent selection of literary fiction, biography, and memoirs. Shopping for food in the Village is an experience that is miles away from pushing your cart through the supermarket. Foodies love the venerable **Murray's Cheese Shop (105)** *(254 Bleecker St., Sixth/Seventh Aves., 212-243-3289, www.murrayscheese.com; hours: M–Sa 8AM–8PM, Su 10AM–7PM),* opened in 1940. For a pound or two of freshly roasted coffee, go to **Porto Rico Importing Co. (106)** *(201 Bleecker St., Sixth Ave./MacDougal St., 212-477-5421, www.portorico.com; hours: M–F 8AM–9PM, Sa 9AM–9PM, Su 12PM–7PM),* a family-owned business that began in 1907. For a taste of high designer fashion, check out **Cynthia Rowley (107)** *(376 Bleecker St., Perry/Charles Sts., 212-242-3803, www.cynthiarowley.com; hours: M–Th*

10AM–8PM, F 10AM–9PM, Sa 11AM–9PM, Su 11AM–8PM) for women's clothing, handbags, eyewear, and shoes. If chess is your game, head to Thompson Street. The **Village Chess Shop (108)** *(230 Thompson St., W. Third/Bleecker Sts., 212-475-9580, www.chess-shop. com; hours: daily 11AM–12AM)* sells chess sets and gives lessons. For the book lover, the world's largest used bookstore, **The Strand Bookstore (109)** *(828 Broadway, corner of E. 12th St., 212-473-1452, www.strandbooks. com; hours: M–Sa 9:30AM–10:30PM, Su 11:00AM–10:30PM, rare book room closes daily at 6:20PM)* is essential browsing. Its motto, before its recent expansion, was "eight miles of books." Now it's "eighteen miles of books."

WHERE TO STAY

It's expensive, but the **Hotel Gansevoort (110) ($$$$)** *(18 Ninth Ave. at W. 13th St., 212-206-6700, www.hotel gansevoort.com)* in the Meatpacking District is a stylish building with generous-sized rooms, a private roof garden, and a pool. The **Washington Square Hotel (111) ($$-$$$$)** *(103 Waverly Place, MacDougal St./Sixth Ave., 212-777-9515, www.wshotel.com)* is a comfortable 100-year old building in a great location across from the square. Rooms aren't big, but it's inexpensive and friendly. The **Larchmont Hotel (112) ($-$$)** *(27 W. 11th St., Fifth/Sixth Aves., 212-989-9333, www.larchmonthotel.com)* is great if you don't mind sharing a bathroom. This small hotel on a beautiful Greenwich Village street has tons of European-style charm: clean, nicely furnished rooms with ceiling fans, and continental breakfast. A tiny town house located in the West Village, the **Abingdon Guest House (113) ($$-$$$)** *(21 Eighth Ave., W. 12th/Jane Sts., 212-243-5384, www.abingdonguesthouse.com)*, is known for its handsomely furnished rooms and quiet, homey atmosphere, but be warned—it has no elevator.

UNION SQUARE

L N Q R 4 5 6 *to 14th St.-Union Square*

● SNAPSHOT ●

Union Square is the city's most historic gathering place. It has been the scene of innumerable labor rallies and war protests and, in the days after September 11, 2001, it was also the site of a moving impromptu shrine. Though there are still protesters, most people come to Union Square these days either to sell vegetables or to buy them; the city's busiest farmer's market is based here. Union Square is also the center of a thriving restaurant-and-hip-hotel scene.

PLACES TO SEE
Landmarks:

On Tuesdays, Thursdays, and Sundays, Union Square is a busy transportation hub, a place to walk the dog and gape at the statues of George Washington, Lafayette, and Gandhi. On Mondays, Wednesdays, Fridays, and Saturdays, the farmers from the surrounding countryside move in. Even if you're not up for food shopping, the **Union Square Greenmarket (114)** *(N. end, Broadway/ Park Ave. S.)* is a good place to spot celebrity chefs, and celebrities shopping for flowers or fruit. In the 1960s, **33 Union Square West (115)** *(near corner of E. 16th St.)* was the home of something far less bucolic: Andy Warhol's Factory.

Those interested in New York history might want to take a look at the **Union Square Theatre (116)** *(100 E. 17th St., at Union Square East, www.nytheatre.com)*. In the 19th century, it was the headquarters of the infamous Tammany Hall, the corrupt political machine that robbed the city coffers, but gave back both Central Park and the Brooklyn Bridge, so perhaps it was a fair exchange.

Arts & Entertainment:

The major draw for most people here is the incredible **Greenmarket (114)** *(see "Landmarks," page 95)*, but if you're a theater fan, you're in luck: the area has two of the hippest and most fun theaters, the **Union Square Theatre (116)** *(100 E. 17th St., Park Ave. S./Irving Pl., www. nytheatre.com)* and the **Daryl Roth Theatre (117)** *(101 E. 15th St. at Union Square East, 212-375-1110, www. darylroththeatre.com)*. Both seem to specialize in putting on experimental and "out-of-the-box" shows (the infamous *De La Guarda*, which ran at the Daryl Roth, for example), full of messy audience participation that kids and teenagers love, though they may well leave theater-goers with more traditional tastes cold. The **Vineyard Theatre (118)** *(108 E. 15th St., 4th Ave./Irving Pl., 212-353-0303, www.vineyardtheatre.org)* also offers adventurous choices; *Avenue Q*, the Tony Award-winning musical, got its start here.

Kids:

Union Square has two playgrounds, enclosed and with safety rubber matting, though they can get pretty crowded. Older kids will enjoy the skateboarding opportunities afforded by the northern end of the square when the Greenmarket is not in operation, which is safely cordoned off from traffic.

PLACES TO EAT & DRINK
Where to Eat:

Eating in this area can be expensive. But good, reasonable, All-American comfort food can be found at **Chat 'n' Chew (119) ($)** *(10 E. 16th Street, Fifth Ave./Union Square West, 212-243-1616, hours: M–F 11AM–12AM, Sa 10AM–12AM, Su 10AM–11PM)*. **15 East (120) ($$$$)** *(15 E. 15th St., Fifth Ave./Union Sq. W, 212-647-0015, www.15eastrestaurant.com; hours: M–F 11:45AM–2PM, 6PM–10:30PM, Sa 6PM–10:30PM)* will satisfy your Japanese cravings—for a pretty penny, but it's worth it. For great Middle Eastern sandwiches, **Rainbow Falafel and Shawarma (121) ($)** *(26 E. 17th St., Fifth Ave./Broadway, 212-691-8641, takeout only; hours: M–Sa 11AM–7PM)* is the place. If you can afford it, Union Square is known for its chic restaurants. The one that started it all is the **Union Square Café (122) ($$$)** *(21 E. 16th St., Fifth Ave./Union Square West, 212-243-4020, www.unionsquarecafe.com; hours: lunch daily 12PM–2:15PM; dinner Su–Th 5:30PM–9:45PM, F–Sa 5:30PM–10:45PM)*. Its friendly service and creative American cuisine make it one of the most popular restaurants in New York. Some other good choices are the **Blue Water Grill (123) ($$$)** *(31 Union Square West. at E. 16th St., 212-675-9500, www.brguestrestaurants.com; hours: lunch M–Sa 11:30AM–4PM; brunch Su 10:30AM–*

4PM; dinner Su–M 5PM–10PM, Tu–Th 5PM–11PM, F–Sa 5PM–12AM; daily dinner service in the Jazz Room starts at 6 PM) for seafood, and **Japonais (124) ($$$)** *(118 E. 18th St., Park Ave./Irving Pl., 212-260-2020, www.japonaisnewyork.com; hours: M–F 12PM–3PM, M–Th 5PM–11PM, F–Sa 5PM–11:30PM)*, which serves high-end Asian fusion in a vibrant atmosphere.

Bars & Nightlife:

If you're a fan of late night talk shows, the **Old Town Bar & Grill (125)** *(45 E. 18th St., Broadway/Park Ave. South, 212-529-6732, www.oldtownbar.com; hours: daily 11:30AM–2AM)* might look familiar: it's featured in the opening credits of *The Late Show with David Letterman*. This 19th-century tavern is a great place to grab a beer and good bar food. **Pete's Tavern (126)** *(129 E. 18th St. at Irving Pl., 212-473-7676, www.petes tavern.com; hours: daily 11AM–2:30AM)* is another old bar: supposedly O. Henry hung out here. For women who love frat boys and the frat boys who love beer,

Heartland Brewery (127) *(35 Union Square West, E. 16th/E. 17th Sts., 212-645-3400, www.heartlandbrewery. com; hours: Su–Th 11:30AM–1AM; F–Sa 11:30AM–2AM)* might do the trick. And if you're looking for some-thing exclusive and quietly hip, go to **Underbar (128)** *(201 Park Ave. South at E. 17th St., 212-358-1560, www.*

gerberbars.com; hours: M–Tu 5PM–3AM, W–F 5PM–4AM, Sa 6PM–4AM, Su 6PM–2AM) inside the trendy **W New York-Union Square Hotel (131)**. **Irving Plaza (129)** *(17 Irving Pl., E. 15th/16 Sts., 212-777-6800, www.irvingplaza.com)* is one of the best rock music clubs in town, host to medium-sized bands and the occasional big name playing a smaller show.

WHERE TO SHOP

For sporting goods, **Paragon Sports (130)** *(867 Broadway at E. 18th St., 212-255-8036, www.paragonsports.com; hours: M–Sa 10AM–8PM, Su 11AM–7PM)* is a local favorite.

WHERE TO STAY

If you don't mind forking out some serious dough, there's always the **W New York-Union Square Hotel (131)** **($$$$)** *(201 Park Ave. South at E. 17th St., 212-253-9119, www.starwoodspecialoffers.com/w_union_square)*. It's housed in a fabulous old building just off Union Square, and has a handsome bar on the ground floor in which to watch the elegant clientele at play.

chapter 4

CHELSEA

GARMENT DISTRICT

TIMES SQUARE-THEATER DISTRICT

& CLINTON

CHELSEA
GARMENT DISTRICT
TIMES SQUARE-
THEATER DISTRICT
& CLINTON

Places to See:

1. Chelsea Hotel
2. 437-459 West 24th Street
3. Cushman Row
4. Starrett-Lehigh Building
5. High Line
6. London Terrace
7. Chelsea Piers
8. Hudson River Park
9. Agora Gallery
10. The Kitchen
11. Museum at the Fashion Institute of Technology
12. Chelsea Art Museum
13. Rubin Museum of Art
14. Joyce Theater
39. Lesbian, Gay, Bisexual & Transgender Community Center
40. Gay Men's Health Crisis
44. Macy's
45. Herald Square
46. Greeley Square
47. Madison Square Garden
48. Penn Station
49. General Post Office
52. New York Times Building (original)
53. New York Times Building (current)
54. NASDAQ Electronic Stock Market Building
55. Reuters Building
56. Condé Nast Building
57. Brill Building
58. Music Row
59. Time & Life Building
60. Lyceum Theatre
61. Ed Sullivan Theater
62. Winter Garden Theater
63. Al Hirschfeld Theater
64. TKTS Booth
65. Times Square Visitors Center
66. Carnegie Hall/Zankel Hall
67. Town Hall
68. Madame Tussauds New York
69. Circle Line
70. Intrepid Sea-Air-Space Museum
71. On Location Tours

CHELSEA

A **C** **E** *to 14th Street;* **C** **E** *to 23rd Street;*
1 *to 18th St. or 23rd St.*

● SNAPSHOT ●

Originally the country estate of a sea captain, Chelsea evolved into a sophisticated urban area with handsome Greek and Italian town houses, great swaths of which still survive and make it one of the most desirable residential areas in the city. Nowadays, Chelsea is primarily renowned for two things that other neighborhoods were once famous for: the gay scene, which has largely migrated from the Village; and the art scene, which became increasingly priced out of Soho. There's also Chelsea's waterfront, which in recent years has seen remarkable development, as have long stretches of the rest of the city's long-neglected waterfront.

PLACES TO SEE
Landmarks:

If it's your first visit to Chelsea, don't miss a visit to the legendary **Chelsea Hotel (1)** *(222 West 23rd St., Seventh/Eighth Aves., 212-243-3700, www.hotelchelsea. com).* This wonderful building with its beautiful rows of cast-iron balconies started life as one of the city's first co-ops, before becoming a hotel in 1905. Its famous clientele has included Tennessee Williams, Mark Twain, Bob Dylan, and Sid Vicious to name a few—but it's far from a museum. It's still a privately operated hotel, and its art-filled lobby and genuinely unconventional clientele offers a real glimpse of pre-Starbucks and chain-store NYC. Check out its basement bar, **Star Lounge** *(212-255-4646, www.starlounge chelsea.com)*, for cocktails and vaguely Eastern stylings. For architecture buffs, two blocks in particular are outstanding for their surviving period details: **437-459 West 24th Street (2)** *(Ninth/Tenth Aves.)*—a row of late Italianate brick houses—and the so-called **Cushman Row (3)** *(406-418 W. 20th St., Ninth/Tenth Aves.)*. On a more modern note, the **Starrett-Lehigh Building (4)** *(601-625 W. 26th St., Eleventh/Twelfth Aves., www.starrett-lehigh building.com)* is one of the city's gems. Designed as a warehouse in 1930-1931, complete with rail tracks leading directly into it, it now leads a less rugged life as home to a cluster of Web designers, media outlets, and the like. It's not a building, but one of Chelsea's most interesting landmarks is the **High Line (5)**, a long-defunct elevated rail track that runs above and just west of Tenth Avenue from around 12th Street to 30th Street, entering and exiting numerous industrial buildings. It has turned into a park and is now an elevated green walkway. Confirming that everything New York is on a grand scale, **London Terrace (6)** *(W. 23rd/W. 24th Sts., Ninth/Tenth Aves., www.londonterracetowers.com)* is a vast apartment building with more than 4,000 rooms occupying an entire square block. Its original developer, who envisioned it as a bastion of British chic complete with doormen dressed as British Bobbies, went bankrupt in the 1930s, and threw himself off the roof. You may see professional dog-walkers and their noisy packs entering or exiting the building. Heading over to the river you'll encounter one of New York's most popular attractions, **Chelsea Piers (7)** *(Piers 59-62, W. 17th/W. 23rd Sts., Eleventh Avenue to the Hudson River, 212-336-6666, www.chelseapiers.com)*, which houses a vast sports complex where you can rock climb, bowl, in-line skate, roller-skate, shoot hoops, and even whack golf balls into a vast net over the Hudson River. There are also a number of bars and restaurants, and fancy docking facilities for the private yachts that berth here. Opinion is divided about all this: some see it as brash commercialism, others as an innovative use of what was once a decaying waterfront that previously offered no access to the public. If Chelsea Piers isn't your thing, you can simply walk or blade away along the waterfront esplanade and park that forms the **Hudson River Park (8)** *(www.hudsonriver park.org)*, which under various guises forms a border of green along most of the west side of Manhattan.

GAY CHELSEA

There are numerous publications that list gay and lesbian events around the city, many of which are free and available in street corner boxes. In particular, check out weeklies *Next* and *Gay City News*. Gay and lesbian visitors can count on the Lesbian, Gay, Bisexual & Transgender Community Center (39) *(208 W. 13th St., Seventh/Eighth Aves., 212-620-7310, www.gaycenter.org),* located slightly south of Chelsea on 13th Street, for information on anything from health issues to simply what's happening around town. More specifically for HIV counseling and advice, there's the venerable Gay Men's Health Crisis (40) *(119 W. 24th Street, Sixth/Seventh Aves., Ste. 6, 212-367-1000, www.gmhc.org).* There are countless bars to suit every taste, but **Barracuda (41)** *(275 W. 22nd St., Seventh/Eighth Aves., 212-645-8613, cash only),* is friendly if too vanilla for some tastes, and **Cafeteria (42)** *(119 Seventh Ave. at 17th St., 212-414-1717, www.cafeteriagroup. com)* is a 24-hour gay-centric restaurant serving a variety of foods from healthy to heavy. If you're looking for a specifically gay place to stay, try the Chelsea Mews Guest House (43) *(344 W. 15th St., Eighth/Ninth Aves., 212-255-9174, cash only).*

Arts & Entertainment:

Chelsea is the commercial art gallery center of New York, and your best bet to appreciate the almost overwhelming scene here is to simply wander up and down Chelsea's streets west of Ninth Avenue: you'll probably discover a show opening. Both established, and emerging art collectors have been visiting the **Agora Gallery (9)** *(530 W. 25th St., 10th/11th Aves., 212-226-4151, www.agoragallery. com; hours: Tu–Sa 11AM–6PM)* since its opening in 1984. It showcases a dynamic range of artists from "around the world and around the corner." **The Kitchen (10)** *(512 W. 19th St., Tenth/Eleventh Aves., 212-255-5793, www.the kitchen.org; hours: Tu–F 12PM–6PM, Sa 11AM–6PM)* is another big Chelsea draw, offering a gallery and a constantly changing series of live performance and video art. The **Museum at the Fashion Institute of Technology (11)** *(Seventh Ave. at W. 27th St., 212-217-4558, www.fitnyc. edu; hours: Tu–F 12PM–8PM, Sa 10AM–5PM)*, an exhibition space attached to this famous powerhouse of New York design, offers immaculately curated shows related to fashion and its social impact. Located in a 30,000-square-foot historic building, the **Chelsea Art Museum (12)** *(556 W. 22nd St., at 11th Ave., 212-255-0719, www.chelseaart museum.org; hours: Tu–W, F–Sa 11AM–6PM, Th 11AM–8PM)* strives to showcase international artists that explore the contemporary human experience. They frequently host artist talks, roundtables, films and performances to foster cross-cultural debate. The **Rubin Museum of Art (13)** *(150 W. 17th St. at 7th Ave., 212-620-5000, www.rmanyc. org; hours: M 11AM–5PM, W 11AM–7PM, Th 11AM–5PM, F 11AM–10PM, Sa–Su 11AM–6PM)* is dedicated to art of the

Himalayas and surrounding areas. Chelsea is more than just art galleries, however, and if you love contemporary dance, the **Joyce Theater (14)** (*175 Eighth Ave. at W. 19th St., 212-242-0800, www. joyce.org*) is not only one of the most beautiful theaters, but also offers some of the most innovative programming, such as the Ballet Hispanico, Savion Glover, and Pilobolus.

PLACES TO EAT & DRINK
Where to Eat:

For reasonably priced Italian, **La Bottega (15)** (**$$**) (*Maritime Hotel, 88 Ninth Ave. at W. 17th St., 212-243-8400, www.themaritimehotel.com; hours: Su–Th 7AM–12AM, F–Sa 7AM–1AM*) is a good bet. With its pretty lanterns and plantings it's easy to forget its outside area is set in the plaza of a hideous 1960s monolith. If you're over by the **Starrett-Lehigh Building (4)** or checking out galleries, **Bottino (16)** (**$$$**) (*246 Tenth Ave., W. 24th/W. 25th Sts., 212-206-6766, www.bottinonyc.com; hours: M 6PM–11PM, Tu–Sa 12PM–3:30PM and 6PM–11PM, Su 6PM–10PM*) is a beautifully minimalist place to stop by for a drink or enjoy a Tuscan meal in one of its two dining rooms. **La Lunchonette (17)** (**$$**) (*130 Tenth Ave. at W. 18th St., 212-675-0342; hours: M–F 12PM–3:30PM and 6PM–11:30PM, Sa–Su 11:30AM–3:30PM and 6PM–11:30PM*) offers delicious French bistro food in a long, low, and intimate setting. At **Salsa y Salsa (18)** (**$$**) (*206 Seventh Ave., W. 21st/W. 22nd Sts., 212-929-2678; hours: daily 12PM–11PM*) you'll find good Mexican standards and great drinks. For classic American fare, you can't beat the **Empire Diner (19)** (**$$**) (*210 Tenth Ave. at W. 22nd St., 212-243-2736, www.empire-diner.com*), open 24 hours a day, and with a great outdoor seating area in warm weather. In a similar vein, try **Better Burgers (20) ($)** *(178 Eighth Ave. at W. 19th St., 212-989-6688, www.betterburgernyc.com; hours: Su–Th 11AM–11PM, F–Sa 11AM–12AM)* for calorie-specific (and antibiotic-free) burgers and fries—you can check out the calorie count of what you're eating on its Web site! For soup and salad lovers, the mini-chain **Hale and Hearty Soups (21) ($)** *(Chelsea Market, 75 Ninth Ave., W. 15th/W. 16th Sts., 212-255-2400, www.haleandhearty. com; hours: M–F 10AM–7PM, Sa–Su 11AM–5PM)* offers tasty and healthy food to go. If you want a tasty burger and fries, hop aboard the **Frying Pan (22) ($)** *(Pier 66, near 26th St. & West Side Highway, 212-362-4453, www.frying pan.com; hours: May–Oct. daily 12PM–12AM)*, an old boat-turned-bar & grill, docked on a railroad car barge at Pier 66.

Bars & Nightlife:

For drinks, **The Half King Bar (23)** *(505 W. 23rd St. at Tenth Ave., 212-462-4300, www.thehalfking.com; hours: break-fast 11AM–11PM, lunch 11AM–4:00PM, dinner 4PM–12AM, late night 12AM–2AM, brunch Sa–Su 9AM–4PM)*, part-owned by author Sebastian Junger, offers perfect pub-grub and pints. **Peter McManus (24)** *(152 Seventh Ave. at W. 19th St., 212-929-9691; hours: M–Sa 11AM–4AM, Su 12PM–4AM)* is a classic no-frills Irish bar, and the **Trailer Park Lounge (25)** *(271 W. 23rd St., Seventh/Eighth Aves., 212-463-8000, www.trailerparklounge.com; hours: daily from 12PM–3AM)* has some frills—if you consider white-trash kitsch a frill, that is. Away from most major residen-tial areas, the far West Side is where many of the city's nightclubs are located. Venues change constantly, so it's best to get one of the many free local publications. **Lotus (26)** (*409 W. 14th St., Ninth/Tenth Aves., 212-243-4420, www.lotusnewyork.com; hours: dining room Tu–Sa 7PM– 11PM, club Tu–Su 10PM–4AM*) is one of the more notorious. If you like velvet ropes and long lines, this is the place for you. Another "scene" can be found at the **Penthouse at the Park (27)** (*118 10th Ave., 17th/18th Sts., 212-352-3313, www.theparknyc.com; hours: F–Sa 12AM–4AM*)—a rooftop patio bar, which boasts a hot tub for its sexy, hip patrons.

WHERE TO SHOP

If you've got the right body (and wallet), Comme des Garçons (28) (*520 W. 22nd St., Tenth/Eleventh Aves., 212-604-9200; hours: M–Sa 11AM–7PM, Su 12PM–6PM*) has those minimalist pants and dresses you desire, and Beatle's daughter Stella McCartney (29) (*429 W. 14th St., Ninth Ave./Washington St., 212-255-1556, www.stellamccartney.com; hours: M–Sa 11AM–7PM, Su 12:30PM–6PM*) has her eponymous boutique here, too. For more affordable stuff, Loehmann's (30) (*101 Seventh Ave., W. 16th/W. 17th Sts., 212-352-0856, www.loehmanns.com; hours: M–Sa 9AM–9PM, Su 11AM–7PM*) offers designer clothes at discount prices. Fittingly located in the art-centric Chelsea, is the bookstore 192 Books (31) (*192 10th Ave., at 21st St., 212-255-4022, www.192books.com; hours: Tu–Sa 11AM– 7PM, Su–M 12PM–7PM*). It often presents art exhibitions coinciding with books relating to the art theme or the artists themselves. For unique furniture, lighting, antique frames, and more, stop by the Hudson City Antiques (32) (*150 9th Ave., 19th/20th Sts., 212-675-8855, www.*

hudsoncityantiques.com; hours: W–Sa 12PM–7PM, Su 12PM–6PM). If you're a jazz fan, the Jazz Record Center (33) *(236 W. 26th St., Seventh/Eighth Aves., 8th floor, 212-675-4480, www.jazzrecordcenter.com; hours: M–Sa 10AM–6PM)* is a real find. Check out the Angel Street Thrift Shop (34) *(118 W. 17th St., 6th/7th Aves., 212-229-0546, www.angelthriftshop.org; hours: M–F 11AM–7PM, Sa 10AM–7PM, Su 12PM–5PM)* for more valuable finds from furniture to fashion. In addition to benefiting your own wardrobe, you'll also be benefiting the community—the shop's proceeds go toward programs for New Yorkers with substance abuse, mental illness, and HIV/AIDS. Considered one of New York's finest vintage shops, the Family Jewels Vintage Clothing (35) *(130 W. 23rd St., 6th/7th Aves., 212-633-6020, www.familyjewelsnyc.com; hours: W–Sa 11AM–8PM, Su–Tu 11AM–7PM)* stocks one-of-a-kind designer fashions and accessories. Chelsea Market (36) *(75 Ninth Ave., W. 15th/W. 16th Sts., www.chelseamarket. com; hours: M–Sa 7AM–10PM, Su 8AM–8PM)* has a wonderful food court that sells everything from freshly baked breads to wine and flowers.

WHERE TO STAY

There's always the Chelsea Hotel (1) ($$–$$$$) *(see "Landmarks," on page 103)* if you think you'll fit the scene, or check out the Chelsea Lodge (37) ($) *(318 W. 20th St., Eighth/Ninth Aves., 212-243-4499, www. chelsealodge.com),* set in a discreet brownstone building, or the Chelsea Star Hotel (38) ($) *(300 W. 30th St. at Eighth Ave., 212-244-7827, www.starhotelny.com),* which offers funky rooms at middling prices, as well as can't-be-beat shared dorms for around $30 a night.

GARMENT DISTRICT

Ⓐ Ⓒ Ⓔ to 34th St.; **① ② ③** to 34th St.-Penn Station;
Ⓑ Ⓓ Ⓕ Ⓜ Ⓝ Ⓠ Ⓡ to 34th St.

● SNAPSHOT ●

Slightly south of **Times Square** *(approximately W. 28th to W. 40th Sts./Sixth to Eighth Aves.)* lies the Garment District, containing New York's clothing industry. You'll know you're there when you stumble upon racks of clothes being wheeled across the street. Take a peep—you're looking at next season's high fashion. You'll also find button, fur, and fabric shops dotted around this neighborhood.

PLACES TO SEE
Landmarks:

The biggest of them all, of course, is **Macy's (44)** *(151 W. 34th St., Broadway/Seventh Ave., 212-695-4400, www.macys.com; hours: M–Sa 10AM–9:30PM, Su 11AM–8:30PM).* From designer clothes to pepper grinders, this block-sized megalith's got it all, as well as a good restaurant for adults and a McDonald's for the kids. Right opposite is **Herald Square (45)** *(1328 Broadway at 34th St.),* and at its southern end **Greeley Square (46)**, which has fairly recently been turned from a shabby no-man's land into an attractive space with tables and chairs in which to take a breather.

Another big landmark in the area is **Madison Square Garden (47)** *(Seventh Ave., W. 31st/W. 33rd Sts., 212-465-6741, www.thegarden.com)*. As New Yorkers love to point out, it isn't on Madison, it isn't a square, and it isn't a garden, but otherwise it lives up to its reputation as "the world's most famous arena," home to pro basketball and hockey games, circuses, concerts, and more. Be warned: basketball tickets for the New York Knicks are almost impossible to get, though you can try the box office on game day. Below the ugly (even New Yorkers admit it) hulk of MSG lies **Penn Station (48)** *(Seventh Ave., W. 31st/W. 33rd Sts.)* an equally unlovely station, built in the '60s on the ashes of the fabulous old station, whose demolition sparked the landmark movement. Fortunately, plans are afoot to restore the magnificent McKim, Mead & White **General Post Office (49)** *(Eighth Ave., W. 31st/W. 33rd Sts.)* nearby, with its massive columned façade, into the new arrival terminal for Penn Station, which will also include links to JFK airport.

WHERE TO SHOP

The Garment District has some good, if not overly flashy shopping options. **Victoria's Secret (50)** *(1328 Broadway at 34th St., 212-356-8383, www.victoriassecret.com; hours: M–Sat 9AM–9:30PM, Su 11AM–8PM)*, that arch purveyor of sexy lingerie, has its flagship store right here in the Garment District, with a huge range of items available. It even offers personalized bra fittings, should you be so inclined. Try **H & M (51)** *(1328 Broadway, at Sixth Ave., 646-473-1165, www.hm.com; hours: M–Sa 9AM–10PM, Su 10AM–9PM)* for trendy, affordable clothes.

A C E *to 42nd St.-Port Authority Bus Terminal;*
N Q R 1 2 3 7 S *to 42nd St.-Times Square*

● **SNAPSHOT** ●

TOP PICK!

In classic New York style, the city's most famous square, ★**TIMES SQUARE** is not a square at all, but the arrowhead where two major thoroughfares—Broadway and Seventh Avenue—meet. In 1905 it acquired its modern name when *The New York Times* newspaper moved uptown to occupy the spot, marking the occasion with a massive New Year's Eve fireworks display that ushered in the role for which the site has become famous. *The New York Times* subsequently decamped to 43rd Street and the old building quickly became a peculiarly American icon as its owners realized it was worth more as a giant billboard than a functioning building. (Today, the area is so well associated with advertising that the Landmarks Commission, in a bizarre ruling, actually requires new buildings in the area to smother their facades with billboards.) With *The New York Times* as its commercial linchpin, theater houses flocked uptown, and by the early 1920s the area had become the city's principal theatrical neighborhood, followed a few years later by the movie theaters. The movie theaters have by and large all gone, but Times Square remains New York's theatrical center, with all the major theaters concentrated on or just off Broadway from the 40s through the 50s. More than 100 years from when the first theaters were built, it's still the place to come to see the latest drama, musical, or revue. Times Square is, of course, famous for its sleaze, and while pockets of XXX-related businesses still linger on (generally west of Eighth Avenue), the past ten years or so have seen a major face-lift and a return—hotly debated by some New Yorkers—to a more family-friendly environment.

PLACES TO SEE
Landmarks:

The New York Times, in its various guises, still dominates the area. Aside from the **original New York Times Building (52)** *(1 Times Square, W. 42nd St., Broadway/Seventh Ave.),* now most famous as the tower from which the New Year's Eve glass ball drops, there's the chateau-style **current New York Times Building (53)** *(217-247 W. 43rd St., Seventh/Eighth Aves.)* that replaced it nearby, which *The New York Times* vacated for a fancy new skyscraper in 2007. Times Square is a cacophony of news and advertising, and no building takes it to more elegant extremes than the **NASDAQ Electronic Stock Market Building (54)** *(Broadway and 43rd St.)* and its amazing eight-story TV screen. Recently, there's been a spate of remarkable new skyscrapers in Times Square, including the **Reuters Building (55)** *(3 Times Square, NE corner of Broadway)* and the **Condé Nast Building (56)** *(4 Times Square, 42nd/43rd Sts.)*, with its elegant stepped façade, home of *The New Yorker* magazine. Times Square was also famous in its day for what was known as Tin Pan Alley, or the pop music business. The center of it was the **Brill Building (57)** *(1619 Broadway at 49th St.)*, where Phil Spector—among many others—worked. It's in the heart of **Music Row (58)** *(48th St., Sixth/Seventh Aves.)* where you'll find plenty of small stores selling guitars and other musical equipment. The **Time & Life Building (59)** *(1271 Sixth Ave., 50th/51st Sts.)* has one of the best public lobbies in the city, complete with works of art.

Arts & Entertainment:

Times Square is all about theater, of course, and the one with the most spectacular Beaux Arts façade is the **Lyceum Theatre (60)** *(149-157 W. 45th St., Sixth/Seventh Aves.)*, which also has a great marble lined interior, complete with murals. Bette Davis and Angela Lansbury, among other stars, performed here. The **Ed Sullivan Theater (61)** *(1697-1699 Broadway, W. 53rd/W. 54th Sts.)* home to David Letterman's *Late Show,* is also a great old theater and a good place to catch stars popping

in and out for the early afternoon tapings of the show. (For tickets, apply at the CBS Web site, www.cbs.com, or visit the theater Monday–Friday, 9:30AM–12PM, weekends 10AM–6PM.) The **Winter Garden Theater (62)** *(1634-1646 Broadway, W. 50th/W. 51st Sts., www.wintergarden-theater.com)* has been home to Al Jolson and the *Ziegfeld Follies* in its past, and now is best known as the place where *Cats* became Broadway's longest-running show. The **Al Hirschfeld Theater (63)** *(302-314 W. 45th St., Eighth/Ninth Aves.),* named after the famed *New York Times* carica-turist, has one of the most knockout interi-ors of all, which alone is worth the price of a ticket. Tickets for these and all other Broadway theaters are most easily purchased online from various ticket brokers, though it's possible to purchase a limited number of day-of-performance tickets from their box offices. Another good place to buy day-of-performance tickets, and at discounts of up to 50%, is the **TKTS Booth (64)** *(center island of W. 47th St., Broadway/ Seventh Aves., www.tdf.org)* in Duffy Square. For more information on where to buy tickets and what's on, visit the indispensable **Times Square Visitors Center (65)** *(on Seventh Ave., W. 46th/W. 47th Sts., www.timessquarenyc.org, M–F 9AM–7PM, Sa–Su 8AM–8PM).* For non-theatrical entertainment, there's **Carnegie Hall (66)** *(154 W. 57th St. at Seventh Ave., 212-247-7800, www.carnegiehall.com),* worth the pilgrimage alone to admire its handsome façade. It also has an excel-lent new performance space beneath it, **Zankel Hall (66)** *(see Carnegie Hall Web site above for details).* For great jazz, cabaret, readings, and more, there's **Town Hall (67)** *(123 W. 43rd St., Broadway/Sixth Ave., 212-840-2824, www.the-townhall-nyc.org)*. If you want something a little different, try **Madame Tussauds New York (68)** *(234 W. 42nd St., Seventh/Eighth Aves., 800-246-8872, www.nycwax.com; hours: Su–Th 10AM–8PM, F–Sa 10AM–10PM)*, where Ozzy Osbourne, Derek Jeter, and other waxen luminaries await. If you like **video games**, then the streets west of Times Square offer a cornucopia of such delights, though the noise can be deafening. The walk west is worth it, though, because it takes you to the pleasures of the waterfront. Not only is there the **Hudson River Park (8)** *(Hudson River to West Side Hwy., Battery Park City to 59th St.)*, with its lovely restored piers, but you can enjoy one of the great tourist pleasures: the **Circle Line (69)** *(W. 42nd St. at Pier 83, Hudson River, 212-563-3200, www.circleline42.com)*. This is a three-hour boat tour around Manhattan, passing underneath all its many bridges, with funny and knowledgeable tour guides who'll turn you into an instant Manhattan expert. Nearby is the **Intrepid Sea-Air-Space Museum (70)** *(W. 46th St. at Pier 86, Hudson River, 212-245-0072, www.intrepidmuseum.org; hours: April 1–Sept 30 M–F 10AM–5PM, Sa–Su 10AM–6PM; Oct. 1–March 31 Tu–Su 10AM–5PM)*, set on the massive bulk of the old *Intrepid* aircraft carrier and full of interactive amusements, two submarines, numerous jet engines, and even a decommissioned Concorde aircraft. Pick up a tour of *New York TV and Movie Sites* from **On Location Tours (71)** *(meeting place near Broadway & 51st St., 212-209-3370, www.screentours.com; call in advance for tickets)* leaving daily at 11AM. You'll see favorite city hotspots from *Seinfeld*, *Friends*, *Sex and the City*, and more.

Kids:

Times Square is now famously family- and kid-friendly since Disney moved in and forced most of the sleaze out. Some New Yorkers carp at this, but one result has been the restoration of two magnificent theaters, the **New Amsterdam Theatre (72)** *(214 W. 42nd St., Seventh/Eighth Aves., www.new-amsterdam-theatre.com)* and the **New Victory Theater (73)** *(209 W. 42nd St., Seventh/Eighth Aves., 646-223-3010, www.newvictory.org)*. The New Amsterdam first premiered the eternally running smash *The Lion King*, while the New Victory is dedicated to children's theatrical shows by visiting companies. There's also **Madame Tussauds (68)** *(see page 118)*, and a gargantuan branch of **Toys "R" Us (74)** *(1514 Broadway, W. 44th/W. 45th Sts., 646-366-8855, www.toysrus.com; hours: M–Th 10AM–10PM, F–Sa 10AM–11PM, Su 10AM–9PM)* which features a 60-foot-high Ferris wheel, a 20-foot-high *T-Rex*, plus a LEGO model of the Empire State Building. It's enough to satisfy any kid. If your kids are adventurous and not too squeamish, you can check out the world of weird and bizarre relics at **Ripley's Believe It or Not! Odditorium (75)** *(234 W. 42nd St., 7th/8th Aves., 212-398-3133, www.ripleysnewyork.com; hours: daily 9AM–1AM)*. Marvel at the unusual artifacts such as shrunken heads, a six-legged cow, and a section of the Berlin Wall.

PLACES TO EAT & DRINK
Where to Eat:

If you're going to a show and in a hurry, there's always **Restaurant Row (76)** *(W. 46th St., Eighth/Ninth Aves.)*. The food is reasonable, and they know you're in a rush, though there are few real surprises here. **Les Sans Culottes (77) ($$)** *(347 W. 46th St., Eighth/Ninth Aves., 212-247-4284; hours: M 4:30PM–10PM, Tu–Sa 11:45AM–3:30PM, 4:30PM–11:30PM, Su 11:30AM–10:30PM)* is good for simple French bistro food, and **Brazil Brazil Churrascaria (78) ($)** *(328 W. 46th St., Eighth/Ninth Aves., 212-957-4300, www.brazilbrazil nyc.com; hours: M–Tu 4PM–12AM, W–Th 12PM–12AM, F–Sa 12PM–1AM, Su 11AM–12AM)* offers tasty steaks in a bright atmosphere with a garden. There's also **Orso (79) ($$-$$$)** *(322 W. 46th St., Eighth/Ninth Aves., 212-489-7212, www.orsorestaurant.com; hours: M, Tu, Th, F 12PM–11:45PM; W, Sa, Su 11:30AM–11:45PM)* for great Italian food, one of the best places on the strip and stuffed with Broadway stars. If you have time, or if you're looking for a more relaxed post-theater meal, venture west to **Clinton** (a.k.a. "Hell's Kitchen") *(40s and 50s west of Eighth Ave.)*, a neighborhood full of great bars and restaurants. There's **Kodama Sushi (80)**

($) *(301 W. 45th St., Eighth/Ninth Aves., 212-582-8065; hours: M–F 12PM–11PM, Sa 12:30PM–11PM, Su 5PM–10PM)* for no-frills sushi in a no-frills space, or low-cost and delicious kosher Israeli food at **Azuri Café (81) ($)** *(465 W. 51st*

St., Ninth/Tenth Aves., 212-262-2920, www.azuricafe. com; hours: Su–Th 10AM–9PM, F 10AM–4PM). New York's famous **Carnegie Deli (82) ($-$$)** (854 Seventh Ave. at 55th St., 212-757-2245, www.carnegiedeli.com; hours: daily 6:30AM–4AM 365 days a year) is cold cut and deli food heaven. Why not indulge in the best of both worlds? Treat yourself to a feast and a treat at **Burgers & Cupcakes (83) ($)** (458 9th Ave., 35th/36th Sts., 212-643-1200, www.burgerscupcakesnyc.com; hours: M–F 8AM–10PM, Sa–Su 11AM–10PM). If you have a hankering for some serious barbeque, head to **Daisy May's BBQ USA (84) ($)** (623 11th Ave., at 46th St., 212-977-1500, www.daisymaysbbq.com; hours: M 11AM–9PM, Tu–F 11AM–10PM, Sa 12PM–10PM, Su 12PM–9PM) for savory, sweet, and down-right delicious fixin's.

Bars & Nightlife:

Pulse Karaoke Lounge (85) (135 W. 41st. St., Sixth Ave./Broadway, 212-278-0090, www.pulsekaroke.com; hours: usually opens daily at 6PM, check Web site), features over 85,000 songs in up to 14 different languages. Special lighting and even gaming stations are available. It's sometimes closed for private parties, so check the Web site for specific opening times. You'll find many bars lining 9th Avenue. Check out the **Mercury Bar (86)** (659 9th Ave., 45th/46th Sts., 212-262-7755, www. mercurybarnyc.com; hours: M–F 11:30AM–4AM, Sa–Su 10:30AM–4AM) to enjoy sports on its big-screen TVs, and its friendly bartenders that will mix up any drink you like!

WHERE TO SHOP

Times Square and its environs is not the most restful area to shop, but many tourists find the bustling **M&M's World (87)** *(1600 Broadway, at 48th St., 212-295-3850, www.mymms.com; hours: daily 10AM–12AM)* a must-stop for their M&M fix. You can create your very own mix of colored candies by using the candy dispensers, and see any of the new flavors on the market. Unique to this New York location, is the 17-foot Green M&M's girl posing as none other than Lady Liberty. A sweet time can be had by all at **Hershey's Times Square (88)** *(1593 Broadway, at 48th St., 212-581-9100, www.hersheys. com; hours: Su–Th 10AM–10PM, F–Sa 10AM–11PM)*. The store celebrates Hershey candies—and you! Visitors can actually see their names go up in lights over Broadway. The **Hell's Kitchen Flea Market (89)** *(W. 39th St. 9th/10th Aves., 212-243-5343, www.hellskitchenfleamarket.com; hours: Sa–Su 9AM–6PM)* is a great place to ferret out a bargain, whether it's a piece of retro clothing or a deco coffee pot, though real bargain hunters get there early!

WHERE TO STAY

Staying at the New York Marriott Marquis Times Square (90) ($$$) *(1535 Broadway, W. 45th/W. 46th Sts., 212-398-1900, www.nymarriottmarquis.com)* hardly feels like being in New York at all, with its L.A.-style valet parking at street level (you have to take an elevator up to reception), and its dizzying James Bond-style central atrium rising 49 floors; however, it's a real trip staying here, and the views from its revolving bar/restaurant are amazing. The Muse (91) ($$$) *(130 W. 46th St., Sixth/Seventh Aves., 212-485-2400, www.themusehotel. com)* may cost a bit, but this is a luxury place that will cosset you perfectly. If you're here for the theater, there's no more convenient place to stay.

chapter 5

FLATIRON DISTRICT & GRAMERCY
MIDTOWN & MURRAY HILL

FLATIRON DISTRICT & GRAMERCY MIDTOWN & MURRAY HILL

Places to See:

1. Madison Square Park
2. Flatiron Building
3. New York Life Insurance Company Building
4. The Players
5. National Arts Club
6. Theodore Roosevelt Birthplace
7. 69th Regiment Armory
8. Augustus Saint-Gaudens Park
28. EMPIRE STATE BUILDING ★
29. Chrysler Building
30. ROCKEFELLER CENTER ★
31. NBC
32. ST. PATRICK'S CATHEDRAL ★
33. Radio City Music Hall
34. Lever House
35. Seagram Building
36. Bryant Park
37. New York Public Library
38. GRAND CENTRAL TERMINAL ★
39. Tudor City
40. United Nations Headquarters
41. The Ford Foundation Building
42. MUSEUM OF MODERN ART (MoMA) ★
43. American Folk Art Museum
44. Paley Center for Media
45. Morgan Library & Museum
46. Scandinavia House
47. Onassis Cultural Center
48. Sony Wonder Technology Lab

Places to Eat & Drink:

10. Craft
11. City Bakery
12. Shake Shack
13. dévi
14. L'Express
15. SushiSamba
16. 71 Irving Place
17. Bamiyan
18. Rodeo Bar
19. Vertigo Bar & Restaurant
50. Burger Heaven
51. Dishes
52. Cosi
53. Alcala
54. Morton's, The Steakhouse
55. Aquavit

★ *Top Picks*

FLATIRON DISTRICT & GRAMERCY

🅕🅜 *to 14th St. or 23rd St.;* 🅛🅝🅠🅡❹❺❻
to 14th St.-Union Square; ❻ *to 23rd St. or 28th St.;*
🅝🅡 *to 23rd St. or 28th St.*

● SNAPSHOT ●

Today, these districts are alike in both being highly "respectable," thriving neighborhoods, full of shops and museums. However, not so long ago the Flatiron District (roughly 14th to 29th streets between Fifth and Park Avenues), and its main public space, Madison Square Park, was a raggedy, crime-ridden sister to neighboring Gramercy Park, which had largely retained its slumbering sense of wealthy calm since the 19th century. A huge face-lift to Madison Square Park and the surrounding areas put an end to this disparity, and now both are essential places on any visitor's itinerary.

PLACES TO SEE
Landmarks:

Like Union Square Park nearby, **Madison Square Park (1)** *(23rd to 26th Sts., Fifth Ave. to Madison Ave.)* has recently seen a reversal of fortune from a drug-plagued place to one where crowds sit, eating lunch during the day, or looking at art exhibits and listening to music on summer nights, thanks to the efforts of the Madison Square Park conservancy *(www.madisonsquarepark.org for*

details). The park has several claims to fame, first as the likely site of the country's first baseball team, the New York Knickerbockers, founded by Alexander Cartwright in 1845, and also as the site of the original Madison Square Garden, long since transferred north to its current site above Penn Station. The two most notable buildings are the **Flatiron Building (2)** *(175 Fifth Ave., 22nd/23rd Sts.),* which gives the neighborhood its name, and the **New York Life Insurance Company Building (3)** *(51 Madison Ave., 26th/27th Sts.).* A gorgeous wedge-shaped 22-story slice of Renaissance terracotta completed in 1903, the **Flatiron Building (2)** gained its name because it was shaped like a clothing iron. At the time, the building's high-rise steel structure was innovative, and it became an instant landmark at the northern end of what was known as "Ladies Mile," the city's most important shopping area. The other great neighborhood edifice, the **New York Life Insurance Company Building (3)** was designed by Cass Gilbert, the same architect who built the Woolworth Building. This lovely 40-story limestone building was built on the site of the original Madison Square Garden. Gramercy Park—unlike Madison Square Park's open-to-all democracy—is based on the English form of a private garden in the center of a square and is only open to residents who have a key, an infinitely prized status object among local residents. Just because you can't get in doesn't mean you shouldn't gaze at the surrounding buildings: there's **The Players (4)** *(16 Gramercy Park S., Park Ave. S./Irving Pl., www.theplayers*

nyc.org), a beautiful Greek Revival town house once owned by famous actor Edwin Booth (his brother shot Lincoln). It is now a private club for men and women in the arts and business. Next door is another famous club, the **National Arts Club (5)** *(15 Gramercy Park S., www. nationalartsclub.org)*, in Gothic

Revival style, where in a suitable boozy atmosphere artists and writers still disport themselves amid walls displaying their art.

Arts & Entertainment:

If you like your museums dimly lit and uncrowded, the wonderful **Theodore Roosevelt Birthplace (6)** *(28 E. 20th St., Broadway/Park Ave. S., 212-260-1616, cash only, www.nps.gov/thrb; hours: Tu–Sa 9AM–5PM)* is for you. Because it's a national historic site (though the original building was demolished in 1916), uniformed Federal Rangers stand guard suspiciously as you peer at the brown furniture and fusty trophy room. Much more modern, at least in spirit, is the **69th Regiment Armory (7)** *(68 Lexington Ave., E. 25th/E. 26th Sts., 212-988-4099)*, host to the original 1913 Armory Show, where cubism and other shocking European phenomena were first unveiled for the American public. Its vast 27,000 square-foot space is host to a number of important arts and antiques fairs during the year.

Kids:

This isn't the most child-friendly of Manhattan neighborhoods, but there's a lovely playground in the Gramercy Park area called the **Augustus Saint-Gaudens Park (8)** *(19th St. at Second Ave.)*. Whether you're an adult or a kid, you'll love Books of Wonder (9) *(18 W. 18th St., Fifth/Sixth Aves., 212-989-3270, www.booksof wonder.net; hours: M–Sa 10AM–7PM, Su 11AM–6PM)*, which stocks childhood classics from *Winnie the Pooh* to *Harry Potter*. It also offers frequent author readings and signings.

PLACES TO EAT & DRINK
Where to Eat:

Craft (10) ($$$) *(43 E. 19th St., Broadway/Park Ave. S., 212-780-0880, www.craftrestaurant.com; hours: M–Th 5:30PM–10PM, F–Sa 5:30PM–11PM, Su 5:30PM–10PM)* is an amazingly minimalist space with simple food—including terrific desserts. **City Bakery (11) ($)** *(3 W. 18th St., Fifth/Sixth Aves., 212-366-1414, www.thecitybakery. com; hours: M–F, 7:30AM–7PM, Sa 7:30AM–6:30PM, Su 9AM–6PM, closes half an hour earlier in summer)* is a neighborhood standard with a great buffet and even better cakes and pastries. If you're in Madison Square Park, don't miss **Shake Shack (12) ($)** *(S. Side Park, near*

Madison Ave./23rd St., 212-889-6600, www.shakeshack nyc.com; daily 11AM–9PM), where you can recover from sightseeing with a hot dog, burger, or ice cream. Over at

dévi (13) ($$) *(8 E. 18th St., Broadway/Fifth Ave., 212-691-1300, www.devinyc.com; hours: lunch M–F 12PM–2:30PM, dinner M–Sa 5:30PM–11PM, Su 5PM–10PM)* there's wonderful Indian food served in a brightly lit, colorful atmosphere. French bistro **L'Express (14) ($$)** *(249 Park Ave. S. at 20th St., 212-254-5858, www.lexpressnyc.com; hours: daily, open 24 hours)* is a locals' favorite, open 24 hours a day, and for something a little more adventurous (and costly) there's **SushiSamba (15) ($$$)** *(245 Park Ave. S., 19th/20th Sts., 212-475-9377, www.sushisamba.com; hours: M–W 11:45AM–1AM, Th–Sa 11:45AM–2AM, Su 11:30AM–12AM)*, a Japanese-South American fusion

restaurant that also serves killer cocktails. For tasty sandwiches and delicious baked goods, try **71 Irving Place (16) ($$)** *(71 Irving Place, E. 18th/19th Sts., 212-995-5252, www.irvingfarm.com; hours: M–W 7AM–11PM, Th–F 7AM–11PM, Sa–Su 8AM–11PM)*. If you've never had Afghan cuisine, you don't know what you're missing. Head to the city's best Afghan restaurant, **Bamiyan (17) ($–$$)** *(358 3rd Ave., at 26th St., 212-481-3232, www.bamiyan.com; hours: daily 12PM–11PM)*, for delicious basmati rice dishes, lamb and chicken kabobs, mild curries, and a variety of dumplings. Don't miss the "Kadu" appetizer—these pumpkin turnovers will melt in your mouth.

Bars & Nightlife:

The **Rodeo Bar (18)** *(375 Third Ave. at 27th St., 212-683-6500, www.rodeobar.com; hours: daily 12PM–2AM)* has a real roadhouse feel to it, complete with country music and sawdust on the floor. It's noisy, has great live music, and

if that's your scene you'll love it. If you prefer a little more of a sleek and sexy scene, **Vertigo Bar & Restaurant (19)** *(354 3rd Ave., at 26th St., 212-696-1011, www. vertigobarnewyork.com; hours: daily 11:30AM–4AM)* will appease your appetite. They've got an assortment of fun cocktail drinks from the *Pear Pom-a-tini* to the *Raspberry Bling*. Live D.J. spinning on Wednesday, Thursday, and Friday nights.

WHERE TO SHOP

Like the raffish English gent look? You can't go wrong shopping at Paul Smith (20) *(108 Fifth Ave. at 16th St., 212-627-9770, www.paulsmith.co.uk; hours: M–W, F–Sa 11AM–7PM; Th 11AM–8PM; Su 12PM–6PM).* Smith's tailored suits, famous striped socks and shirts, and super-cool shoes can't be beat. If you're a music lover, Academy Records (21) *(12 W. 18th St., Fifth/Sixth Aves., 212-242-3000, www.academy-records. com; hours: daily 11AM–7PM)* has an amazing jazz and classical collection in both vinyl and CD format in a browserfriendly environment. Don't worry about the weird name—**Fishs Eddy (22)** *(889 Broadway at E. 19th St., 212-420-9020, www.fishseddy.com; hours: M 10AM–10PM, Tu–Sa 9AM–10PM, Su 10AM–9PM)* is a mini-chain that offers irresistible china and glassware from overstocked corporations, factories, and out-of-business restaurants. Each plate tells a story. And it's cheap—you'll walk out with twice what you expected to buy. **ABC Carpet & Home (23)** *(888 Broadway at E. 19th St., 212-473-3000, www.abchome.com; hours: M–Sa 10AM–7PM, Su 11AM–6:30PM)* is famous for its huge selection of home furnishings, decorations, and bazaar-like atmosphere.

WHERE TO STAY

Indulge yourself with a stay at the luxurious **Hotel Giraffe (24) ($$$-$$$$)** *(365 Park Ave. S. at 26th St., 877-296-0009, www.hotelgiraffe.com)*. The design throughout is inspired by the 1920s and '30s, with rich lavish colors and textures creating a sophisticated, yet comfortable setting. Amenities include all the cappuccino, espresso, cookies and fruit that you can eat all day, to keep your energy flowing as you explore this non-stop, vibrant city. Complimentary breakfast buffet included, as well as a selection of champagne, wine and cheese to wind down your day while you listen to live cocktail piano music. Ian Schrager has transformed the **Gramercy Park Hotel (25) ($$$$)** *(2 Lexington Ave. at 21st St., 212-920-3300, www.gramercyparkhotel.com)* into an elegantly modern oasis, combining different styles of furniture, art, and rich colors to create a diverse, sensuous setting. There is a lovely private roof club with a bar and landscaped garden.

MIDTOWN & MURRAY HILL

B D F M to 42nd St.-Bryant Park or
47th-50th Sts.-Rockefeller Center; S 4 5 6 7 to
Grand Central-42nd St.; N R Q to Fifth Ave.-59th St.;
E M to Fifth Ave.-53rd St.

● SNAPSHOT ●

When visitors think of New York, the first images that come to mind are usually the iconic ones of its famous skyscrapers, in all their Deco glory, rising high above the bustling streets. This is Midtown, the place that for many—New Yorkers and tourists alike—epitomizes the city. It's here that Fifth Avenue swells to its most majestic state. The Empire State Building, Chrysler Building, Rockefeller Center, and United Nations complex, to name just a few, ascend skywards, and Radio City Music Hall, Tiffany's, the Plaza Hotel, Saks, and a host of other New York institutions made familiar through a million TV shows and movies, can be found here. It's no wonder that a first-time visitor's impression is often: *Haven't I seen all this before?* Murray Hill, a highly fashionable residential area in lower Midtown, contains some remarkable buildings (in particular a number of lovely carriage houses now converted to residences), as well as restaurants and shops. It's not quite as electric as Midtown (what is?), but it's a pleasant and rewarding neighborhood to venture into if you wish to lower the street energy for a while.

PLACES TO SEE
Landmarks:

Perhaps the most famous address in the world, **Fifth Avenue** was originally a residential street for the ultra-wealthy, before becoming one of the city's most prestigious commercial strips as the big stores began to move north from 34th Street. Some of the original private mansions were later converted into shops. Cartier Inc. (26) *(Fifth Ave. at 52nd St., 212-753-0111, www. cartier.com; hours: M–Sa 10AM–6PM, Su 12PM–5PM),* the jewelers, now occupies one of the greatest Renaissance mansions on Fifth Avenue; and Versace (27) *(647 Fifth Ave., 51st/52nd Sts., 212-317-0224, www.versace.com; hours: M–Sa 10AM–7PM, Su 12PM–6PM)* occupies a former Vanderbilt mansion next door. Skyscrapers are what the neighborhood is famous for, and the ★EMPIRE STATE BUILDING (28) *(350 Fifth Ave., 33rd/34th Sts., 212-736-3100, www.esbnyc.com; hours: observatory open 8AM–2AM daily, last elevators go up at 1:15AM)* is the most famous of all, immortalized in films such as *When Harry Met Sally* and *An Affair to Remember.* At 1,250 feet, it beat out the spanking new Chrysler Building for crown of tallest building in the world when it opened in 1931.

TOP PICK!

The sights from its 86th floor viewing level are amazing. (Note that with new security measures, it can take *a long time* to get up there.) Admission tickets can also

be purchased for the 102nd floor observatory. It may be a touch shorter, but the **Chrysler Building (29)** *(405 Lexington Ave., 42nd/43rd Sts.; hours: M–F 8:30AM– 5:30PM)*, with its great gargoyles and Deco detailing, is far more romantic and has an infinitely richer public lobby.

TOP PICK!

★**ROCKEFELLER CENTER (30)** *(Fifth to Sixth Aves., 48th/51st Sts., 212-632-3975, www.rockefeller*

center.com) is a collection of 19 buildings—both office and commercial space—a sunken shopping plaza, and an open-air public plaza, all brilliantly arranged in harmony with each other. Work began in the 1930s and was extended until the early

1950s. The Top of the Rock observation deck offers great views of New York City, and you'll find all kinds of adventures within the complex. **NBC (31)** *(30 Rockefeller Plaza, 49th St., Fifth/Sixth Aves., call 212-664-3700 for tour info, www.nbc.com)* is a tenant. There's also good shopping in the plaza above and below, and a wonderful **Rink at Rockefeller Center** for ice-skating, open October to April *(call 212-332-7654 for prices and hours)*. Rockefeller Plaza is the site of New York City's Christmas tree and its celebrity lighting each year.

TOP PICK! On a less secular level, there's **★ST. PATRICK'S CATHEDRAL (32)** *(Fifth Ave., E. 50th/E. 51st Sts., 212-753-2261, www.saintpatrickscathedral.org; hours: 6:30AM–8:45PM daily)* nearby, a Gothic masterpiece where the hush once inside its vast doors makes a lovely contrast to the perpetual bustle outside. It is the largest Gothic Catholic cathedral in North America and seat of the archbishop of the Roman Catholic Archdiocese of New York. **Radio City Music Hall (33)** *(1260 Sixth Ave., W. 50th/W. 51st Sts., 212-247-4777, www.radiocity.com)* remains one of the great architectural and theatrical gems of the city. Today, it's best known for its annual Christmas extravaganza with the high kickin' Rockettes. You can take in its sumptuous interior, without paying for a show, by joining one of its regular behind-the-scenes tours. If you like your architecture modern, a little farther north is the famous **Lever House (34)** *(390 Park Ave., E. 53rd/E. 54th Sts.)*—an International Style stainless steel and glass curtain-walled office building that inspired a million knockoffs. The other classic International Style skyscraper is the **Seagram Building (35)** *(375 Park Ave., E. 52nd/E. 53rd Sts.)*, a sleek, almost ominous, glass and bronze-framed tower designed by Mies van der Rohe and Philip Johnson. Between West 40th and West 42nd streets on the east side of Sixth Avenue lies **Bryant Park (36)** *(www.bryantpark.org)*, one of the loveliest public spaces in the city. In warm weather you can pull up a chair and sit on the graveled walkways pretending you're in the Tuileries. The park is behind the majestic **New York Public Library (37)** *(476 Fifth Ave., W. 42nd to 40th Sts., 917-275-6975, www.nypl.org; call or visit Web site for hours)*, a Beaux Arts masterpiece with its famous twin lions guarding the entrance. The Rose Reading room is worth a visit, and there are usually excellent free exhibitions, too. Eastward lies ★**GRAND CENTRAL TERMINAL (38)** *(E. 42nd to E. 44th Sts., Vanderbilt to Lexington Aves., 212-340-2583, www.grandcentral terminal.com)*, one of New York's greatest landmarks, which was saved from demolition and is now beautifully restored inside. The expanded terminal had opened in 1913 and was a hub for area redevelopment until World War II. Years of disrepair followed, until famous New Yorkers like Jacqueline Kennedy Onassis took up the cause. Check out its famous painted ceiling of the constellations. As part of the restoration, there's also a terrific (but expensive) food market on the main level and a (much cheaper) food court on the lower level *(see pages 144 and 148)*. Head toward the East River and you'll encounter **Tudor City (39)** *(E. 40th St. to E. 43rd St., First/Second Aves., www.tudor city.com)*, a fascinating 1920s Tudor-style collection of apartment buildings funded by Rockefeller alongside what was once the city's busiest slaughterhouse area. They form an enclave of peace and quiet from busy

TOP PICK!

Second Avenue, and nestling in the middle is a delightful and beautifully maintained public park. Nearby, in high-modern style lies the **United Nations Headquarters (40)** *(E. 42nd to E. 48th Sts., First Ave./FDR Dr., 212-963-8687 for tour info, www.un.org; hours: guided tours M–F 9:45AM–4:45PM)*, where you technically leave U.S. soil as you enter. **The Ford Foundation Building (41)** *(321 E. 42nd St., First/Second Aves.)*, with its incredible atrium that is visible from both the street and offices, is arguably the finest postwar building in New York. It's one of the great public spaces in the city and you just know it costs a bundle to keep all those delicate trees alive.

Arts & Entertainment:

Midtown has some excellent museums, including the 630,000-square-foot ★**MUSEUM OF MODERN ART (MoMA) (42)** *(11 W. 53rd St., Fifth/Sixth Aves., 212-708-9400, www.moma.org; hours: Su–M, W, Th, Sa 10:30AM–5:30PM, F 10:30AM–8PM)*. Its white walls and pure spaces are home to a permanent collection by the likes of Matisse, Picasso, Pollock, and Warhol, and it features major exhibitions as well. MoMA "seeks to create a dialogue between the established and the experimental, the past and the present," according to its literature. It's a whopping $20 for admission, but few complain once they've seen the incredible collection of visual media inside. It also has arguably the best gift shop of any

TOP PICK!

museum in the city. Less famous is the **American Folk Art Museum (43)** *(45 W. 53rd St., Fifth/Sixth Aves., 212-265-1040, www.folkartmuseum.org; hours: Tu–Su 10:30AM–5:30PM, F 11AM–7:30PM)*, housing a delightful collection of early Americana, paintings, signboards, quilts, and the like, as well as temporary exhibitions. And its magnificent award-winning bronze-plated façade makes it equally as deserving of all the hyperbole lavished on the **MoMA (42)**. The **Paley Center for Media (44)** *(25 W. 52nd St., Fifth/Sixth Aves., 212-621-6800, www.mtr.org; hours: W, F–Su 12PM–6PM, Th 12PM–8PM)* provides curated shows on particular themes such as Hollywood or an individual performer, as well as artifacts and screenings from all ages of the American entertainment industry. *(See also page 142.)* The venerable **Morgan Library & Museum (45)** *(225 Madison Avenue, at 36th St., 212-685-0008, www.themorgan.org; hours: Tu–Th 10:30AM–5PM, F 10:30AM–9PM, Sa 10AM–6PM, Su 11AM–6PM)* was the original home of the uber-robber baron, financier J. P. Morgan, and along with his magnificent library, you can see Morgan's jaw-dropping collection of Italian Renaissance paintings and sculpture. Two other places to view interesting exhibitions are the **Scandinavia House (46)** *(58 Park Ave., 37th/38th Sts., 212-879-9779, www.scandinaviahouse.org; hours: Tu–Sa 12PM–6PM)* and the **Onassis Cultural Center (47)** *(645 5th Ave., entrance on 51st St., 212-486-4448, www.onassis usa.org; hours: M–Sa 10AM–6PM)*. Both have free admission.

Kids:

The **Paley Center for Media (44)** *(see also page 141)* offers a wonderful series of workshops entitled "Recreating Radio" *(call 212-621-6600 for details),* in which kids, aged nine and up, collaborate to make an old-fashioned radio serial program, complete with scripts, sound effects, and editing. Afterward, they get to take away a recording of their labors. For the tech-enthusiast among your kids, you can't beat the **Sony Wonder Technology Lab (48)** *(56th St. at Madison Ave., 212-833-8100, http://wondertechlab.sony.com; hours: same day tickets are available on a first come, first serve basis beginning at 10AM Tu–Sa and 12PM Su)*—four floors of interactive fun, including a 73-seat HDTV viewing theater, where you and your kids can make music, video, and film clips, explore computers, and much more. If your little darlings are demanding toys, sate 'em at **FAO Schwarz (49)** *(767 Fifth Ave., 58th/59th Sts., 212-644-9400, www. fao.com; hours: Su 11AM–6PM, M–Th 10AM–7PM, F–Sa 10AM–8PM),* a vast palace of toys, utterly addictive to any child.

PLACES TO EAT & DRINK
Where to Eat:

For a quick and cheap burger fix, there's **Burger Heaven (50) ($)** (*20 E. 49th St., Fifth/Madison Aves., 212-755-2166, www.burgerheaven.com; hours: M–F 7AM–7:30PM, Sa*

8AM–5:45PM, Su 9:30AM–4:30PM)—rushed, but tasty. For sandwiches, soups, and salads (weekdays only) that are heads and shoulders above the average, **Dishes (51) ($)** (*6 E. 45th St., Fifth/ Madison Aves., 212-687-5511; hours: M–F: 7AM–5PM*) is the place to go. The **Cosi (52) ($)** (*60 E. 56th St., Madison/Park Aves., 212-588-1225, www.getcosi.com; hours: M–F 6:30AM–8PM, Sa–Su 7:30AM–8PM*) chain of sandwich shops is also a good cheap bet. If you want to splurge more and you like tapas and Basque food, **Alcala (53) ($$)** (*342 E. 46th St., First/ Second Aves., 212-370-1866, www.alcala restaurant.com; hours: M–Th 12PM–2:30PM, 5:30PM–10PM, F 12PM–2:30PM, 5:30PM–11PM, Sa–Su 5:30PM–9PM*) is excellent. For a serious carnivorous session, **Morton's, The Steakhouse (54) ($$$–$$$$)** (*551 Fifth Ave. at 45th St., 212-972-3315, www.mortons.com; hours: M–F 11:30AM–11PM, Sa 5:30PM–11PM, Su 5PM–10PM*) can't be

beat. Scandinavian food is on the rare side in New York, but **Aquavit (55) ($$$–$$$$)** (*65 E. 55th St., Madison/Park Aves., 212-307-7311, www.aquavit.org; café hours: M–Th lunch 12PM–2:30PM, dinner 5:30PM–10:30PM; F, Sa lunch*

12PM–2:30PM, dinner 5:30PM–10:45PM; Su dinner 5:30PM–10:30PM; dining room hours: M–Th lunch 12:30PM–2:20PM, dinner 5:30PM–10:30PM) wows even jaded city palates. Be treated to an insider's view of Japan at **Aburiya Kinnosuke (56) ($$-$$$)** *(213 E. 45th St., at 3rd Ave., 212-867-5454, www.aburiya kinnosuke.com; hours: M–F 11:30AM–2:30PM, 5:30PM–11PM, Sa 5:30PM–11PM, Su 5:30PM–10:30PM)*. A unique and fun experience, diners have the option of grilling their own dishes right at their tables. The **Delegates' Dining Room (57) ($$)** *(UN, 4th floor, First Ave. at 46th St., 212-963-7626, www.delegates diningroom.com; hours: M–F 11:30AM–2:30PM, reservations required for the public at least 24 hours in advance)* at the United Nations has the most eclectic clientele by far of any restaurant in the city, and offers amazing river views with its weekday-only lunch buffets. You're advised to reserve. Finally, Grand Central Terminal is home to the **Grand Central Oyster Bar (58) ($$)** *(see Grand Central Terminal in "Landmarks," on page 139, www.oysterbarny.com; hours: M–F 11:30AM–9:30PM, Sa 12PM–9:30PM)* in its lower level, where you can pig out on oysters and clam chowder in an elegant and truly iconic New York City space. The lower level food court also has a large array of cheaper fast food options.

Bars & Nightlife:

The King Cole Bar at the St. Regis Hotel (59) *(2 E. 55th St., Fifth/Madison Aves., 212-339-6857, www.kingcolebar.com; hours: M–Th 11:30AM–1AM, F–Sa 11:30AM–2AM, Su 12PM–12AM)* is *waaay* expensive, but the clubby armchairs, wooden paneling, and Maxfield Parrish mural behind the bar of King Cole himself make it worth every cent. Just as pricey is the **Oak Room at the Algonquin Hotel (60)** *(59 W. 44th St., Fifth/Sixth Aves., 212-840-6800, www.algonquinhotel. com; hours: Tu–Sa by reservation only)*, where there's great jazz and a darkened atmosphere. As dark and historic as these two but far more democratic, **P. J. Clarke's (61)** *(915 Third Ave at 55th St., 212-317-1616, www.pjclarkes.com; hours: daily kitchen 11:30AM–3AM, bar 11:30AM–4AM)* offers beer, music, and comfort food. **The Campbell Apartment (62)** *(15 Vanderbilt Ave., 42nd/43rd Sts., 212-953-0409, www.hospitality holdings.com; hours: M–Th 12PM–1AM, F 12PM–2AM, Sa 3PM–2AM, Su 3PM–11PM)* is a 1920s-era section of Grand Central Terminal, complete with 25-foot-high ceilings, that serves up jazz, cocktails, and a general Deco sensibility. **Nikki Midtown (63)** *(151 E. 50th St., Lexington/Third Aves., 212-753-1144, call for hours)* is part of the nightclub chain Nikki Beach, established in warm-weather venues such as Miami and St. Bart's. For un-ashamed hipsters there's **Whiskey Blue (64)** *(541 Lexington Ave. at 49th St., 212-407-2947; hours: M–Tu 4:30PM–3AM, W–Th, 4:30PM–3AM, F 4:30PM–4AM,*

Sa 6PM–4AM, Su 6PM–2AM), part of the trendy W Hotel. For unabashed nostalgia lovers there's **Bill's Gay Nineties (65)** *(57 E. 54th St., Madison/Park Aves., 212-355-0243, www.billsnyc.com; hours: lunch: M–F 11:30AM–4:30PM, dinner: M–Sa 5PM–11:30PM),* a piano bar that began life as a speakeasy in 1930. In Murray Hill, **Artisanal (66)** *(2 Park Ave. at 32nd St., 212-725-8585; hours: M 11:45AM–10PM, Tu–F 11:45AM–11PM, Sa 5PM–11PM, Su 5PM–10PM)* is a great bar and restaurant where cheese and wine rule. The folks here are serious about

their tasting pleasures, and will help you find just the right fromage to go with that special glass of wine. If you're a foodie, this place is a must. **Les Halles (67)** *(411 Park Ave. South, E. 28th/E. 29th Sts., 212-679-4111, www.leshalles.net; hours: daily 7:30AM–12AM)* is celeb chef Anthony Bourdain's famous bar/restaurant, where a slick and well-heeled crowd tuck into brasserie food with gusto. If you want a more casual experience here, simply sit at the bar with a drink and enjoy the excellent people-watching. **Joshua Tree (68)** *(513 Third Ave., E. 34th/E. 35th Sts., 212-689-0058, www. joshuatreebar.com; hours: M–F 11AM–4AM, Sa–Su 10AM–4AM)* is a neighborhood institution for no particular reason other than that it's simply there. But it's a good and friendly place to drop by for a beer or two, and its young crowd is both well-educated and easy on the eye.

WHERE TO SHOP

A landmark since 1902, Saks Fifth Avenue (69) *(611 Fifth Ave. at 50th St., 212-753-4000, www.saks.com; hours: M–Sa 10AM–8PM, Su 12PM–7PM)* is one of the greatest of all New York's department stores and it's great for men's and women's clothes, jewelry, perfumes, and gifts. Call for details of its regular trunk shows. Just as smart is Bergdorf Goodman (70) *(754 Fifth Ave., 57th/58th Sts., 212-753-7300, www.bergdorfgoodman.com; hours: M–F 10AM–8PM, Sa 10AM–7PM, Su 12PM–6PM)*, where you'll see fur-coated ladies who lunch while checking out the jewelry and shoes. Prices are steep, though the seasonal sales offer genuine bargains. Think you can't afford something at Tiffany & Co. (71) *(727 Fifth Ave, 56th/57th Sts., 212-755-8000, www.tiffany.com; hours: M–Sa: 10AM–7PM, Su: 12PM–6PM)*? Well, there are a few things the average purse can handle, including a silver bookmark (in that quintessential little blue box), and a few other items "under $175," as its Web site puts it. For high fashion there's Gucci (72) *(725 Fifth Ave., at 56th St., 212-826-2600, www.gucci.com; hours: M–Sa 10AM–8PM; Su 12PM–6PM)*, a place where you will either

 feel entirely at home or run screaming through the door, depending on your tastes. At Chanel (73) *(15 E. 57th St., Fifth/Madison Aves., 212-355-5050, www.chanel.com; hours: M–W, F 10AM–6:30PM, Th*

10AM–7PM, Sa 10AM–6PM, Su 12PM–5PM) you can pick up a lipstick for a mere $20, or a suit for $2,000 and up. If you just want good, honest, no-nonsense, relatively inexpensive men's clothes there's always Brooks Brothers (74) *(1270 Sixth Ave. at Rockefeller Center, 212-247-9374, www.brooksbrothers.com; hours: M–F 8AM–9PM, Sa 9AM–8PM; Su 10AM–7PM)*. For literary types there's Bauman Rare Books (75) *(535 Madison Ave., 54th/55th Sts., 212-751-0011, www.baumanrarebooks.com; hours: M–Sa 10AM–6PM)*, where first editions rule and you can ogle such beautiful bound editions as an original *Alice in Wonderland* or Darwin's *Origin of the Species*. For food, there's Grand Central Food Market (76) *(see Grand Central Terminal in "Landmarks," on page 139)*, which has great delectables, particularly its meat, fish, and selection of fabulous cheese, as well as gift items such as chocolates and flowers. The lower level of Rockefeller Center (30) *(see Rockefeller Center in "Landmarks," on page 137)* offers a whole range of gifts and clothes, from smart designer apparel to basic tee shirts and jeans.

chapter 6

LINCOLN CENTER & ENVIRONS
UPPER WEST SIDE

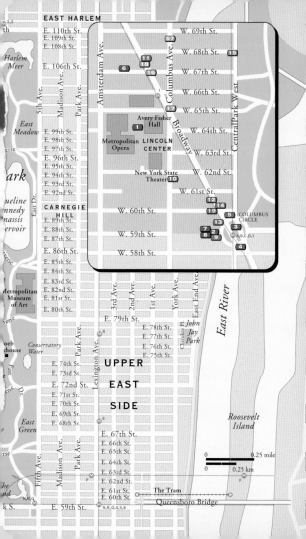

WHERE TO STAY

After a busy day of sight-seeing, rest your weary head on one of the variety of pillow styles available at the graceful and stylish **70 Park Avenue Hotel (77) ($$$$)** *(70 Park Ave., at 38th St., 212-973-2400, www.70parkave.com).* This hotel is also pet-friendly if you don't want to leave Fido at home. **Hotel 31 (78) ($)** *(120 E. 31st St., Park Ave. S./Lexington Ave., 212-685-3060, www.hotel31.com)* is grungier, but at around $85 a night and up, it's hard to complain. Money no object? You can't beat the **Waldorf-Astoria Hotel (79) ($$-$$$)** *(301 Park Ave., at 50th St., 212-355-3000, www.waldorfastoria.com)*—a Deco masterpiece where Frank Sinatra, Diana Ross, and a host of other well-known performers have entertained diners. The lobby's worth a look even if you aren't staying there. A much more reasonable option is the **Pod Hotel (80) ($$)** *(230 E. 51st St., Second/Third Aves., 212-355-0300, www.thepodhotel.com)*, with shared bathrooms for a number of rooms.

LINCOLN CENTER & ENVIRONS
UPPER WEST SIDE

Places to See:

1. Lincoln Center for the Performing Arts
1. Metropolitan Opera House
1. New York State Theater
1. Walter Reade Theater
1. Film Society of Lincoln Center
2. Time Warner Center
3. Columbus Circle
4. Museum of Arts and Design
6. Merkin Concert Hall
7. Frederick P. Rose Hall
8. Dizzy's Club *Coca-Cola*
20. Ansonia Hotel
21. Central Park West
22. The Dakota
23. San Remo Apartments
24. Congregation Shearith Israel
25. Pomander Walk
26. Riverside Drive
27. Riverside Park
28. West 79th Street Marina and Boat Basin
29. American Museum of Natural History/ Rose Center for Earth and Space
30. Beacon Theatre
31. Symphony Space
32. El Taller Latino Americano
33. New-York Historical Society
34. Children's Museum of Manhattan

Places to Eat & Drink:

9. Per Se
10. Rosa Mexicano
11. Ollie's
12. Sapphire Indian Cuisine
13. Stone Rose Lounge
14. Gabriel's Bar
15. Vince & Eddie's
35. Big Nick's Burger & Pizza Joint
36. Josie's Restaurant
37. Café Blossom
38. Café Lalo
39. Alice's Tea Cup
40. Boat Basin Café
41. Café Luxembourg
42. Gray's Papaya
43. Bistro Citron
44. Carmine's
45. Mamá Mexico
46. Buceo 95
47. Underground Lounge

LINCOLN CENTER & ENVIRONS

1 *to 66th St.-Lincoln Center;*
A C B D 1 *to 59th St.-Columbus Circle*

● SNAPSHOT ●

The neighborhood around the Lincoln Center for the Performing Arts was originally part of Clinton, its neighbor to the south. Both areas were collectively known as "Hell's Kitchen," a vital, working-class neighborhood that sprawled westward to the Hudson and was infamous for its gangs and crime. Then in the early 1960s gentrification arrived in the newly minted form of "urban renewal," and the crumbling brownstones filled with lonely studios were converted back to family use again or demolished in great swaths to make way for—among other things—places such as Lincoln Center. The site is filled with venues, including the Metropolitan Opera House, New York State Theater, and the Avery Fisher Hall. Individually they're a fairly loveless group of buildings, but their saving grace is the wonderful main public plaza that unites them, and on a summer's night when the fountains are flowing there's no more magical spot to be in New York.

PLACES TO SEE
Landmarks:

Lincoln Center for the Performing Arts (1) *(W. 62nd to W. 66th Sts., Columbus/Amsterdam Aves., 212-546-2656 for event listings, www.lincolncenter.org)* is most impressive at night, when the buildings and fountain are all lit up—it's a fun spot to just hang out and watch New York's ceaseless street parade. In the summer there's dancing in the plaza (see "Midsummer Night Swing" on its Web site). For individual attractions, see "Arts & Entertainment," page 155. The other major landmark here is the dynamic **Time Warner Center (2)** *(SW side of Columbus Circle., 58th/59th Sts., www.shopsatcolumbus circle.com)*, a twin-towered glass monolith that rises far above everything else. Inside its shiny 2.8-million square foot, $1.7-billion interior is a mini-city in itself, consisting of a hotel, condos, shops, restaurants, corporate headquarters, and more. *(See "Where to Shop," "Places to Eat & Drink," and "Arts & Entertainment.")* Everyone agreed that Columbus Circle needed a new building that would make a statement and help define this awkward circle-in-a-grid space, but its glossy opulence tends to polarize opinion: you'll either love it or hate it.

Dwarfed by this building is the statue of Columbus perched on his column in the center of **Columbus Circle (3)**, hand on hip as though in defiance at all that's going on around him. On the far side of Columbus Circle is the "lollipop building," originally designed as the **Gallery of Modern Art**

now the **Museum of Arts and Design (4)** *(2 Columbus Circle, Broadway/Eighth Ave., 212-299-7777, www.mad museum.org; hours; Tu–Su 11AM–6PM, Th 11AM–9PM)* showcasing crafts, arts, and design. You can't explore New York without encountering mega-developer Donald Trump's influence. Years ago he took over the old 44-story Gulf and Western building, had it re-clad at vast expense by architect Philip Johnson, and— voila!—the **Trump International Hotel & Tower (5)** *(1 Central Park West at Columbus Circle, 212-299-1000, www.trumpintl.com)* was born. The building is home to supermodels and baseball players, and anyone else who can afford the rent.

Arts & Entertainment:

Lincoln Center for the Performing Arts (1) *(see page 154)* is New York's altar of high culture, and whether it's ballet, opera, symphonic music, or film, you'll find it here at its finest. The **Metropolitan Opera House (1)** *(212-362-6000, www.metopera.org)* is the flashiest Lincoln Center building, located right in front of the plaza's main fountain, and offers a wide range of operas—from *Tosca* and *La Boheme*, that an operatic novice will enjoy, to more esoteric fare. It has an excellent and informative Web site. The Met's own company is in residence September through May, and touring companies perform in the summer. The **New York State Theater (1)** houses the **New York City Ballet** *(www.nycballet.com, 212-870-5570)* and the **New York City Opera** *(www.nycopera.com),* which is cheaper than the Met, and offers the opportunity to spot rising talent in the making before they become more expensive to catch. The **Walter Reade Theater (1)** *(212-875-5600, www.filmlinc.com, cash only at the box office)* is home to the **Film Society of Lincoln Center (1)**, which sponsors the annual New York Film festival, as well as offering year-round viewings of films not otherwise available, plus revivals and directors' talks. A block away from all this high-brow activity is the excellent and quirky **Merkin Concert Hall (6)** *(Kaufman Center, 129 W. 67th St., Broadway/Amsterdam Ave., 212-501-3330, www.kaufman-center.org),* which features jazz, experimental music, live broadcasts, and family theater matinees. The **Time Warner Center (2)** *(see "Landmarks," on page 154)* has several cultural hot spots, most notably the **Frederick P. Rose Hall (7)** *(Broadway at 60th St., 5th floor, 212-258-9800, www.jazzatlincolncenter.com),* a stunning glass-backed auditorium with amazing acoustics and sweeping views of Manhattan in the background. It hosts Lincoln Center's annual Jazz Festival, among other events. **Dizzy's Club** *Coca-Cola* **(8)** *(www.jazzatlincolncenter.com)* is a more intimate retro-style jazz club, also on the fifth floor, that holds just 140 people.

PLACES TO EAT & DRINK
Where to Eat:

There's a cluster of restaurants and watering holes in the **Time Warner Center (2)** *(see "Landmarks," on page 154),* including **Per Se (9) ($$$-$$$$)** *(4th floor, 212-823-9335, www.perseny.com; hours: lunch F–Su 11:30AM–*

1:30PM, dinner M–Su 5:30PM–10PM), ace chef Thomas Keller's fancy joint, which currently has about a two-month waiting list but which is, according to the chosen few who've gained entry, the best restaurant in New York. Lincoln Center is, of course, surrounded by restaurants, and **Rosa Mexicano (10) ($$$)** *(61 Columbus Ave. at W. 62nd St., 212-977-7700, www.rosamexicano. com; hours: M 11:30AM–10:30PM, Tu–F 11:30AM–11:30PM, Sa 11:30AM–2:30PM, 4PM–11:30PM, Su 11:30AM–2:30PM, 4PM–10:30PM)* offers fantastic Mexican food and great drinks. On the cheaper side, try **Ollie's (11) ($-$$)** *(1991 Broadway, W. 67th/W. 68th Sts., 212-595-8181; hours: daily 11:30AM–11:30PM)* for fast yet tasty Chinese food. For a calmer environment than most around here, there's **Sapphire Indian Cuisine (12) ($$)** *(1845 Broadway, W. 60th/W. 61st Sts., 212-245-4444, www.sapphireny.com; hours: M–Sa 11:45AM–2:45PM, M–Th 5PM–10:30PM, F–Sa 5PM–11:00PM, Su 5PM–10:30PM)*, which also offers a great low-cost lunch.

Bars & Nightlife:

The **Time Warner Center (2)** *(see "Landmarks," on page 154)* offers a number of night life opportunities, the fanciest being Rande Gerber's **Stone Rose Lounge (13)** *(10 Columbus Circle, 4th floor, 212-823-9769, www. gerberbars.com; hours: daily 4PM–2AM)*.
The views of Central Park at night are pretty cool, and who knows—you may even bump into some celebrities. **Gabriel's Bar (14)** *(11 W. 60th St., Columbus Ave./*

*Broadway, 212-956-4600, www.gabrielsbarandrest.com;
hours: M–F lunch and dinner, Sa dinner only)* is a no-pretense Italian restaurant, with wonderful cozy booths in which to pull up at night for a few post-show drinks. **Vince & Eddie's (15)** *(70 W. 68th St., Columbus Ave./Central Park West, 212-721-0068, www.vinceand eddiesnewyork.com; hours: M–W 11:30AM–3PM, 4:30PM–10PM, Th–F, 11:30AM–3PM, 4:30PM–12AM; Sa 10:30AM–3PM, 4:30PM–12AM, Su 10:30AM–3PM)* is another restaurant that's great for drinks, and has a secret garden and romantic fireplaces. There's live classical music on the weekends.

WHERE TO SHOP

The **Time Warner Center (2)** *(see "Landmarks," on page 154)* has a collection of high-class stores, if money is no object, including **Swarovski**—for a crystal souvenir that will really sparkle. For lesser mortals there's always **J. Crew**, **Coach**, **Williams-Sonoma**, and the like. The **Whole Foods** supermarket here is the largest in New

York, 59,000 square feet of impeccably displayed and carefully chosen goods, along with a cafe and a sushi bar. If you love beauty products, the **Sephora** chain has a small branch here offering Pop, Stila, and other cosmetic brands with unusually friendly service for a beauty joint. For household items there are two trusty stalwarts nearby, **Pottery Barn (16)** *(1965 Broadway at W. 67th St., 212-579-8477, www.potterybarn.com; hours: M–Sa 10AM–9PM, Su*

11AM–7PM) and Bed Bath & Beyond (17) *(1932 Broadway at W. 65th St., 917-441-9391, www.bedbath andbeyond.com; hours: daily 9AM–10PM).* There's also Gracious Home (18) *(1992 Broadway at 67th St., 212-231-7800, www.gracioushome.com; hours: M–F 9AM–8:30PM, Sa 9AM–9PM, Su 10AM–7PM),* which, as its name implies, has hardware and housewares to grace your home.

WHERE TO STAY

The area immediately around Lincoln Center is expensive, and you might want to consider moving a few blocks uptown to some of the Upper West Side's less expensive hotels *(see page 169).* But if you do want to stay right by all the cultural action there's the Mandarin Oriental New York (19) *($$$$) (80 Columbus Circle at W. 60th St., 212-805-8800, www.mandarinoriental.com),* part of the Time Warner complex; it offers amazing park views and prices to match. Or try the Trump International Hotel & Tower (5) *($$$$) (1 Central Park West at Columbus Circle, 212-299-1001, www.trumpintl.com),* which will lighten your wallet even more.

UPPER WEST SIDE

B **C** to 72nd St., 81st St., 86th St., 96th St., 103rd St., Cathedral Parkway-110th St.; **1** to 79th St., 86th St., 96th St., 103rd St.; **2** **3** to 72nd St., 96th St.

● SNAPSHOT ●

The Upper West Side is the traditional liberal and intellectual heart of Manhattan, home to prominent museums and a wealthy, sophisticated populace. There's an endless and ongoing rivalry with the Upper East Side's denizens across the park, who are perceived by some to be more conservative, though the staggering escalation of real estate values and development in the West Side during the past few years has done much to blur this traditional boundary. It's *Seinfeld* territory, of course, and if Midtown is the iconic center of Manhattan with its skyscrapers, then the Upper West Side is the "regular guy" residential center of Manhattan for all those who aren't downtown-chic or Upper East Side-loaded: single or married with kids, this is where you come to live what passes for the "normal" life in Manhattan. As a result, it's a great place to explore for its vast array of restaurants, wonderful human-scaled side streets, and, of course, easy access to New York's great gem, Central Park, the development that brought the Upper West Side into being as a residential neighborhood in the first place during the late 19th century.

PLACES TO SEE
Landmarks:

The **Ansonia Hotel (20)** *(2109 Broadway, W. 73rd/W. 74th Sts., www.ansoniacondo.com)* is an amazing Beaux Arts building that is actually an apartment building, not a hotel. Its developer was a stickler for quality construction, including soundproof partitions, which resulted in numerous musicians living there, including Caruso and Stravinsky. Later it helped drown out the cries from Plato's Retreat, a notorious 1970s swinger club located there. **Central Park West (21)**, one of New York's most desirable addresses, runs up the west side of Central Park and is home to some of the finest residential buildings in the city. **The Dakota (22)** *(1 W. 72nd St. at Central Park West)* is probably the most famous of them, former home to John Lennon and current home of his widow, Yoko Ono. Hard to imagine it was once one of the sole buildings in a remote neighborhood when completed in 1884— hence its joking name, which stuck. If you look at Central Park West from Central Park, the Italian Renaissance-style twin towers of the **San Remo Apartments (23)** *(145-146 Central Park West, W. 74th/75th Sts.)* are among the most iconic. Bono bought a little pad in one of them for around $15 million, joining a nest of other celebs there—a tough thing to do, considering Madonna was turned down by its co-op board. There are numerous religious and cultural institutions along Central Park West, and one of the handsomest is **Congregation Shearith Israel (24)** *(8 W. 70th St., www.shearith-israel.org)* a synagogue masquerading as a Georgian-style porticoed temple, built at the turn of the 19th century. The lovely brownstone residential blocks between the park and the Hudson River are well worth exploring. Pick a random route and you'll come across all sorts of unexpected architectural treats. One of the loveliest is **Pomander Walk (25)** *(W. 94th/W. 95th Sts., Broadway/ West End Aves.),* an English-style mews of cottages running only one block and which creates a delightful mini-village atmosphere. **Riverside Drive (26)** *(W. 72nd St. to Fort Tryon Park)* is the other great residential address on the West Side, a majestic sweep that runs along the Hudson River and can best be appreciated from the water *(see Circle Line Cruises in "Times Square" on page 118).* It's home to a combination of the old-moneyed intelligentsia and, increasingly, celebrities. Much of its charm derives from **Riverside Park (27)** *(W. 72nd St. to W. 153rd St., www.river*

sideparkfund.org), which runs next to it along the river, and is a brilliantly landscaped creation of Frederick Law Olmsted, co-creator of Central Park. Make note to see the **West 79th Street Marina and Boat Basin (28)**

(Hudson River at W. 79th St.), where a number of hardy souls, including entire families with children, live year round on houseboats. There's also an excellent cafe there *(see **Boat Basin Café (40)** on page 165).*

Arts & Entertainment:

The "big daddy" of museums here is the **American Museum of Natural History (29)** *(main entrance Central Park West at W. 79th St., 212-769-5100, www.amnh. org; hours: daily 10AM–5:45PM),* which stretches alongside Central Park between W. 77th and W. 81st streets. There are endless models and skeletons of dinosaurs, reptiles, and fish, as well as changing exhibits, an IMAX theater, and countless buttons to push. The museum is also home to the **Rose Center for Earth and Space (29)**, a planetarium in an astounding glass box that will whisk you away on virtual reality tours to Mars and beyond. It's not to be missed. If you love live music, the Upper West Side is home to the **Beacon Theatre (30)** *(2124 Broadway, W. 74th/W. 75th Sts., 212-465-6500, www.beacontheatre.com)* a mid-sized venue originally built in 1928 as a vaudeville palace that plays host to lesser-known acts and huge acts like the Stones and Bob Dylan when they want to play in more intimate venues. **Symphony Space (31)** *(2537 Broadway at W. 95th St., 212-864-5400, www. symphonyspace.org)* offers offbeat performance art of all kinds, including an excellent film, dance, literature, and film series, plus family theater events. At **El Taller Latino Americano (32)** *("The Latin American Workshop")*

(2710 Broadway at W. 104th St., 212-665-9460, www.tallerlatino.org) you'll find classes and workshops from flamenco dancing to guitar playing, as well as frequent visits by Latino arts organizations. The **New-York Historical Society (33)** *(170 Central Park West at 77th St., 212-873-3400, www.nyhistory.org; hours: Tu–Th, Sa 10AM–6PM, F 10AM–8PM, Su 11AM–5:45PM)* is a treasure trove of reading material and historical collections, including John James Audubon watercolors.

Kids:

The **Children's Museum of Manhattan (34)** *(212 W. 83rd St., Broadway/Amsterdam Aves., 212-721-1223, www. cmom.org; hours: Tu–Su 10AM–5PM)* is a terrific resource for kids, offering play areas, drawing and music classes, workshops, interactive exhibits, and more. The loud and very fabulous **Big Nick's Burger & Pizza Joint (35) ($)** *(2175 Broadway at 77th St., 212-362-9238, www.bignicksnyc.com; hours: daily 24 hours)* is great for kids. The name says it all.

PLACES TO EAT & DRINK
Where to Eat:

Get your organic fix at **Josie's Restaurant (36) ($$)** *(300 Amsterdam Ave., at 74th St., 212-769-1212, www.josies nyc.com; hours: M–F 12PM–10:30PM, Sa 11AM–10:30PM, Su 10:30AM–10PM)*, where you'll find healthful, wholesome, (and yes, delicious!) New American cuisine. Eating healthy and consciously never tasted so good at the organic vegan restaurant **Café Blossom (37) ($$)** *(466 Columbus Ave., 82nd/83rd Sts., 212-875-2600,* *www.blossomnyc.com; hours: M–F 11AM–10PM, Sa 11AM–10:15PM, Su 11AM–9:15PM).* Even non-vegans will be tempted by the diverse and creative menu. The soy bacon cheeseburger with caramelized onions and chipotle aioli is divine. **Café Lalo (38) ($-$$)** *(201 W. 83rd St., Amsterdam Ave./ Broadway, 212-496-6031, www. cafelalo.com; hours: M–Th 8AM– 2AM, F 8AM–4AM, Sa 9AM–4AM, Su 9AM–2AM)* is brightly lit and crowded, but good for coffee and desserts. If you're an Anglophile, **Alice's Tea Cup (39) ($-$$)** *(102 W. 73rd St., Amsterdam/Columbus Aves., 212-799-3006, www.alicesteacup.com; hours: daily 8AM–8PM)* is the perfect place, with its cozy atmosphere and 200 blends of tea. The **Boat Basin Café (40) ($$-$$$)** *(W. 79th St. at the Hudson River, 212-496-5542, www.boatbasincafe.com; hours: M–W 12PM–11PM, Th–F 12PM–11:30PM, Sa 11AM–11:30PM, Su 11AM–10PM)* has great views and some of the best and most friendly barbecues in the city. **Café Luxembourg (41) ($$$)** *(200 W. 70th St., Amsterdam/Columbus Aves., 212-* *873-7411, www.cafeluxembourg.com; hours: M–Tu 8AM–11PM, W–F 8AM–12AM, Sa 9AM–12AM, Su 9AM–10PM)* is a neighborhood classic. Great bistro food, very stylish, and always crowded. Love hot dogs and a bargain? **Gray's Papaya (42) ($)** *(2090 Broadway at W. 72nd St., 212-799-0242; hours: daily 24 hours)* can't be beat for its delicious dogs and cool fruit drinks. Heading uptown a bit, **Bistro Citron (43)** **($–$$)** *(473 Columbus Ave., W. 82nd/W. 83rd Sts., 212-400-9401, www.bistrocitronnyc.com; hours: M–Sa 12PM–11PM, Su 11AM–10PM)* offers French comfort foods. Long-time favorite **Carmine's (44) ($$)** *(2450 Broadway, W. 90th/W. 91st Sts., 212-362-2200, www.carminesnyc.com; hours: Su–Th 11:30AM–11PM, F–Sa 11:30AM–12AM)* is for really pigging out on huge portions of basic Italian; best for groups and family outings. Family-operated **Mamá Mexico (45) ($$)** *(2672 Broadway at 102nd St., 212-864-2323, www.mamamexico.com; hours: M–Th, Su 12PM–12AM, F–Sa 12PM–2AM)* treats its patrons to Mexican regional specialty dishes "with an accent of Mayan culture." Try

the Salmón Cozumel—grilled salmon topped with a chipotle-honey barbecue sauce—paired with their Rainbow Margarita. Live Mariachi band performs daily.

Bars & Nightlife:

If you want to take a trip to Barcelona, without leaving the Upper West Side, head to **Buceo 95 (46)** *(201 W. 95th St., at Amsterdam Ave., 212-662-7010, www.buceo95.com; hours: Su–Th 5PM–12AM, F–Sa 5PM–2AM)* for tapas and wine. The **Underground Lounge (47)** *(955 West End Ave., at 107th St., 212-531-4759, www.theundergroundnyc.com; hours: daily 4PM–4AM)* hosts comedy shows, live music, and "Salsa Tuesdays." **Compass (48)** *(208 W. 70th St., Amsterdam/West End Aves., 212-875-8600, www. compassrestaurant.com; hours: Su–Th 5PM–10PM, F–Sa 5PM–11PM)*, a French-American bar and restaurant,

brings a generally absent minimalist chic to this neck of the woods. Founded by soul duo Ashford & Simpson, **Sugar Bar (49)** *(254 W. 72nd St., Broadway/West End Ave., 212-579-0222, www.sugarbarnyc.com; hours: Tu–W 5PM–11PM, Th–Sa 5PM–1AM)* is a great African-themed bar with live soul and jazz and a reasonable cover. It also does a gospel brunch on Sundays. **Nice Matin (50)** *(201 W. 79th St. at Amsterdam Ave., 212-873-6423; hours: M 7AM–11PM, Tu–F 7AM–12AM, Sa 10:30AM–12AM, Su 10;30AM–11PM)* has a bizarre decorative scheme of warring colors and patterns, but the wide range of beers and wines by the glass will make you forget all that. The **Abbey Pub (51)** *(237 W. 105th, near corner of Broadway, 212-222-8713; hours: M–Th 4PM–2AM, F 2PM–4AM, Sa–Su 4PM–4AM)* is the place for you if you take your drinking seri-

ously. Beers, burgers, and three TV screens for watching sports make it a favorite local spot. Beware the more exotic fare on the menu.

You can't say you've been to the Upper West Side till you've been to Zabar's (52) *(2245 Broadway at W. 80th St., 212-787-2000, www.zabars.com; hours: M–F 8AM–7:30PM, Sa 8AM–8PM, Su 9AM–6PM)*, a food-cum-household appliance store that has amazing prices and

great quality. Avoid coming on the weekend at all costs. H & H Bagels (53) *(2239 Broadway at W. 80th St., 212-595-8000, www.hhbagels.com; hours: daily 24 hours)* was founded in 1972 and is the most famous bagel maker in the world, helped along by mentions on *Friends* and *Seinfeld*. It's open 24 hours. For a trifecta of food shopping classics, check out Barney Greengrass (54) *(541 Amsterdam Ave., W. 86th/W. 87th Sts., 212-724-4707, www.barneygreengrass.com; hours: T–Su 8AM–6PM)* with its pricey but fabulous sturgeon, lox, bialys, and more. For clothes try Barneys Co-Op (55) *(2151 Broadway at W. 75th St., 646-335-0978, www.barneys.com; hours: M–F 10AM–8PM, Sa 10AM–7PM, Su 11AM–6PM)*, a hipper, edgier spinoff of the main Barneys store on Madison Avenue. *(See the Upper East Side's "Where to Shop," on page 182.)* For women's clothes there's the ever-playful Betsey Johnson (56) *(248 Columbus Ave., W. 71st/W. 72nd Sts., 212-362-3364, www.betseyjohnson. com; hours: M–Sa 11AM–7PM, Su 12PM–7PM)* for fun, flirty dresses

chapter 7

UPPER EAST SIDE
CENTRAL PARK

and the like. Robert Marc (57) *(190 Columbus Ave., W. 68th/W. 69th Sts., 212-799-4600, www.robertmarc.com; hours: M–F 10AM–7PM, Sa 10AM–6PM, Su 12PM–6PM)* has several stores around town offering some seriously cool spectacles. Finally, just want to look without (probably) buying? Maxilla & Mandible (58) *(451 Columbus Ave., W. 81st/W. 82nd Sts., 212-724-6173, www. maxillaandmandible.com; hours: M–Sa 11AM–7PM, Su 1PM–5PM)* is where the young Indiana Jones in the making goes for his animal and fish skeletons. Bizarre but fun.

WHERE TO STAY

The Amsterdam Inn (59) ($) *(340 Amsterdam Ave. at W. 76th St., 212-579-7500, www.amsterdaminn.com)* offers 30 rooms, with both shared and private baths, all at reasonable rates. On the Ave Hotel (60) ($$) *(2178 Broadway at W. 77th St., 212-362-1100, www.ontheave-nyc.com)* is a mid-priced hotel with great views of Central Park and more style than many hotels in this neighborhood.

UPPER EAST SIDE
CENTRAL PARK

Places to See:

Places to Eat & Drink:

Where to Shop:

Where to Stay:

④⑤ to 59th St. or 86th St.; **⑥** to 59th St., 68th St.,
77th St., 86th St., 96th St., 103rd St., 110th St.;
ⓃⓇⓆ to Fifth Ave.-59th St., Lexington Ave.-59th St.

● **SNAPSHOT** ●

The Upper East Side is an astonishingly varied and rich
(in every sense of the word) part of the city. A brief stroll
around the ritzier stretches of Fifth or Madison Avenues
will certainly reveal more than a fair share of frosty
blondes with Pekinese in tow or imperious old ladies
being helped out of taxis by obsequious doormen, but
it's much more than that. The stretches east of
Lexington Avenue ("The East Upper East Side") resem-
ble the Upper West Side in their relatively democratic
social make-up. There is also the cultural bounty of the
area to consider: "Museum Mile" with its amazing cluster of world-class museums, and some of the most
mouth-watering architecture in the city.

PLACES TO SEE
Landmarks:

The heart of chic and moneyed
New York is the so-called "**Gold
Coast,**" which runs for about a
mile between E. 60th and E. 80th
streets from Fifth Avenue to Park
Avenue. This was the area where
the gilded-age robber barons built

their new park-side mansions when Central Park came into being. Many of these buildings have since been converted either to apartments or consulates. One of the most amazing is **11 E. 62nd Street (1)** *(Fifth/Madison Aves.)*, a former private mansion now home to Japan's UN representative. The opulence of its limestone façade and Beaux Arts details still amazes today in a world of Donald Trump high-rises. Another example is **11 E. 73rd St. (2)** *(Fifth/Madison Aves.)*, originally the Joseph and Kate Pulitzer House (of Pulitzer Prize renown), now converted into apartments. Around the turn of the 19th century the rich began to leave their beautiful, yet hard-to-keep-up, mansions and moved to the latest architectural invention—the apartment building. Naturally they sacrificed nothing in terms of style, as the **45 East 66th Street Apartments (3)** *(Madison/Park Aves.)* demonstrate. With its lovely Gothic details and large windows it's as desirable a residence today as it was nearly 100 years ago. With an average per-resident income of around $200,000 a year (south of E. 96th Street, that is), Park Avenue deserves its wealthy reputation. Yet its secret is that it is actually built over railroad tracks that had been an open trench and eyesore for many years until they were covered over around the turn of the century. At E. 96th Street, Park Avenue's little secret emerges from underground and the character of the street and the surrounding neighborhood changes drastically. It's fun to watch the trains come crawling out of the dark here. Along the waterfront there's **Carl Schurz Park (4)** *(East River between E. 84th/E. 90th Sts., www.carlschurzparknyc.org)*, a beautifully designed park built out ingeniously over the FDR Drive below. It affords amazing views across to Queens on the other side. The park contains the Mayor's official residence, **Gracie Mansion (5)** *(E. 88th St. at East End Ave., 212-570-4751; hours: tours offered W 10AM, 11AM, 1PM, 2PM)*, Manhattan's sole remaining Federal-style house, which is now open to the public, though you must reserve ahead of time for tours.

The designation "Upper East Side" incorporates several other residential areas that are worth exploring, including **Carnegie Hill** *(E. 86th to E. 96th Sts., Fifth/Third Aves.)* and **Yorkville** *(E. 72nd to E. 96th Sts., Central Park/East River)*. Both are filled with elegant tree-lined streets and fine shops and restaurants. Carnegie Hill in particular is home to a number of superb museums, including the **Jewish Museum (6)** *(1109 Fifth Ave. at E. 92nd St., 212-423-3200, www.thejewishmuseum.org: daily 11AM–5:45PM, 8PM on Th, closed W)*; the **Solomon R. Guggenheim Museum (7)** *(1071 Fifth Ave. at E. 89th St., 212-423-3500, www.guggenheim.org; hours: F, Su–W 10AM–5:45PM, Sa 10AM–7:45PM)*; and the **Cooper-Hewitt National Design Museum (8)** *(2 E. 91st St. at Fifth Ave., 212-849-8400, www.cooperhewitt.org; hours: M–F 10AM–5PM, Sa 10AM–6PM, Su 11AM–6PM)*, which was converted from steel magnate Andrew Carnegie's private 1902 mansion, and ignited development in this area at the time. Yorkville became a notably German neighborhood, and the wealthy Rhinelander family in particular built many beautiful mansions and apartment buildings here in conjunction with architect Henry Hardenbergh, designer of the Dakota Building. The most famous of these is the **Rhinelander Mansion (9)** *(867 Madison Ave., E. 71st/E. 72nd Sts.),* a stunning building, both inside and out, that's now home to Ralph Lauren's Polo empire in New York.

Arts & Entertainment:

The Upper East Side is high-brow heaven, with the greatest concentration of museums in the city. **"Museum Mile"** is the name given to the stretch of cultural institutions that runs along Fifth Avenue from E. 82nd to E. 104th streets. The biggest and most famous of them all is the ★METROPOLITAN MUSEUM OF ART (10) *(1000 Fifth Ave. at E. 82nd St., 212-535-7710, www.metmuseum.org; hours: Tu–Th 9:30AM–5:30PM, F–Sa 9:30AM–9PM, Su 9:30AM–5:30PM),* a vast treasure house that runs four blocks north up Fifth Avenue and expands deeply into Central Park at the back. The Met's slogan is "5,000 years of art," and they aren't kidding; walking into its vast central rotunda with galleries radiating off it can be intimidating. The permanent collection offers something for everyone, from paintings to photographs to musical instruments to textiles. Each month brings special exhibitions. It's best to choose a particular part— European painting, Egyptian art—and enjoy it in detail rather than attempt the impossible and try to "see it all." On Fridays and Saturdays the Met hosts a string quartet and cocktails upstairs, which is expensive but one of the best people-watching events in the city—look out for all those nervous first daters. From classical temple to out-

TOP PICK!

rageous modern swirl, the **Solomon R. Guggenheim Museum (7)** *(1071 Fifth Ave. at E. 89th St., 212-423-3500, www.guggenheim.org; hours: F, Su–W 10AM–* *5:45PM, Sa 10AM–7:45PM)* couldn't be more different from the Met. Its circular concrete structure that seems to twist itself out of the ground is architect Frank Lloyd Wright's most iconic structure. Inside, this spiral is even more amazing, though opinion is divided about how successful a space it is to actually view the modern art on exhibit there. Farther north is the **Cooper-Hewitt National Design Museum (8)** *(2 E. 91st St. at Fifth Ave., 212-849-8400, www.cooperhewitt.org; hours: M–F 10AM–5PM, Sa 10AM–6PM, Su 11AM–6PM)*, a handsome limestone-clad building that's dedicated to the history of design, both domestic and industrial. Expect to find exhibitions covering eclectic subject matter from wallpaper to silverware to classic 1960s road maps, to name but a few recent ones. The **Jewish Museum (6)** *(1109 Fifth Ave. at E. 92nd St., 212-423-3200, www.thejewishmuseum.org: daily 11AM–5:45PM, 8PM on Th, closed W)* is housed in a 1908 chateau and has a large permanent collection of artifacts related to Jewish life and culture, in addition to hosting impressive temporary exhibitions. There's also a kosher cafe. The **National Academy Museum (11)** *(1083 5th Ave., at 89th St., 212-369-4880. www.national academy.org)* promotes American art through exhibitions and houses one of the largest public collections of 19th and 20th century art in the U.S. At the time this book went to press, the museum was closed for renovation. Check Web site for updates. The **Neue Galerie (12)** *(1048 5th Ave., at 86th St., 212-628-6200, www. neuegalerie.org; hours: Th–M 11AM–6PM)*, housed in an historical landmark building designed by Carrère & Hastings, displays early 20th-century German and Austrian art and design pieces. Off Museum Mile are a few other major museums, including the **Whitney Museum of American Art (13)** *(945 Madison Ave. at E. 75th St., 212-570-3600, www.whitney. org; hours: W–Th 11AM–6PM, F 1PM–9PM, Sa–Su 11AM–6PM)*. Its fortress-like façade puts many off, but inside there's a plethora of amazing art, by such artists as Edward Hopper, Willem de Kooning, and Georgia O'Keeffe. Far more sedate is the **Frick Collection (14)** *(1 E. 70th St., Fifth/Madison Aves., 212-288-0700, www.frick.org; hours: Tu–Sa 10AM–6PM, Su 11AM–5PM)*, a charming classical mansion once owned by industrialist Henry Clay Frick. It has a garden surrounding it, an indoor pond, and a terrific collection of old masters, including Vermeer, Van Dyke, and Rembrandt. Finally, there's the **Asia Society and Museum (15)** *(725 Park Ave. at E. 70th St., 212-288-6400, www.asiasociety.org; hours: Tu–Su 11AM–6PM)*, housed in a sleek modern building with a spacious

 interior that does justice to the delicacy of the works on display. There's an Asian restaurant attached where the food is artfully prepared and just as pleasing to the taste buds.

Kids:

Carl Schurz Park (4) *(East River between E. 84th/E. 90th Sts.)* is wonderful for children, in particular the playground at E. 84th Street and
East End Avenue. **EJ's Luncheonette (16)** *(1271 Third Ave. at E. 73rd St., 212-472-0600: M–Sa 8AM–11PM, Su 8AM–10:30PM)* is loud, kid-friendly, and cheap. Jacadi (17) *(1242 Madison Ave. at E. 89th St., 212-369-1616, www.jacadiusa.com; hours: M–Sa 10AM–6PM, Su 12PM–5PM)* offers French clothes if you want to make your baseball cap-wearing little darling look more Euro.

PLACES TO EAT & DRINK
Where to Eat:

The Upper East Side doesn't boast the array of top-class restaurants that Downtown does. With some notable exceptions, the area is full of "local favorites"—good but not overly exciting. One of those exceptions is **Serendipity3 (18) ($$)** *(225 E. 60th St., 2nd/3rd Aves., 212-838-3531, www.serendipity3.com; hours: Su–Th 11:30AM–12AM, F 11:30AM–1AM, Sa 11:30AM–2AM)*. It holds a Guinness World Record for the most expensive sundae—coming in at $1000—it's covered in edible gold leaf. But what people really come here for is the famous "Frrrozen Hot Chocolate." Although it's typically known for its desserts, they make a mean burger. Be prepared to wait for a table. **Daniel (19) ($$$$)** *(60 E. 65th St., Madison/Park Aves., 212-288-0033, www.danielnyc. com; hours: M–Th 5:45PM–11PM, F–Sa 5:30PM–11PM)* is an institution for contemporary

French cuisine. For good burgers and other American fare there's **Jackson Hole (20) ($$)** *(232 E. 64th St, Second/Third Aves., 212-371-7187, www.jacksonhole burgers.com; hours: M–Th 10:30AM–1AM, F–Sa 10:30AM–1:30AM, Su 10:30AM–12AM)*. In the 70s there's **Due (21) ($$)** *(1396 Third Ave., E. 79th/E. 80th Sts., 212-772-3331, cash only; hours: Su–Th 12PM–12AM, F–Sa 12PM–1AM)* for good Northern Italian. For tasty Southwestern cuisine try **Cilantro (22) ($$)** *(1321 First Ave., at 71st St., 212-537-4040, www.cilantronyc.com; hours: M–Sa 11AM–12AM, Su 11AM–11PM)*. The atmosphere is charming and the margaritas will knock you off your socks. In the 80s there's **Beyoglu (23) ($$)** *(1431 Third Ave. at E. 81st St., 212-650-0850; hours: Su–Th 12PM–11PM, F–Sa 12PM–12AM)*, an excellent Mediterranean-Turkish place where the best thing to do is share a bunch of the fresh appetizers. If you fancy some star-spotting with your Italian-American food try **Elaine's (24) ($$$)** *(1703 Second Ave., E. 88th/E. 89th Sts., 212-534-8103; hours: M–Sa 6PM–2AM, Su 5PM–1AM)*. A remnant of the old German community in Yorkville is **Heidelberg (25) ($$)** *(1648 Second Ave., E. 85th/E. 86th Sts., 212-628-2332, www.heidelberg restaurant.com; hours: daily 11:30AM–10PM)*, which has kitschy décor but solid portions. In the 90s, try **Vico (26) ($$$)** *(1302 Madison Ave., E. 92nd/E. 93rd Sts., 212-876-2222, cash only; hours daily 12PM–3PM, 5PM–11PM)* if you want to splurge on really good Italian food. An unusual Brazilian outpost up here is **Zebú Grill (27) ($$)** *(305 E. 92nd St., First/Second Aves., 212-426-7500, www.zebugrill.com; hours: Su–Tu 5PM–11PM, W–Sa*

5PM–11:30PM), which offers a really lively vibe, especially for this neighborhood, and truly flavorful food.

Bars & Nightlife:

Stir (28) *(1363 First Ave. at E. 73rd St., 212-744-7190; hours: Su–W 5PM–1AM, Th 5PM–2AM, F 5PM–3AM, Sa 5PM–4AM)* is an exposed-brick minimalist bar that claims to "bring the flavor of Downtown to the Upper East Side." Far more old-school is **Harry Cipriani (29)** *(781 Fifth Ave., E. 59th/E. 60th Sts., 212-753-5566, www.cipriani.com; hours: daily 7AM–12AM)*, where waiters in tuxes create a potentially daunting atmosphere for some, though it's a true New York experience. **Club Macanudo (30)** *(26 E. 63rd St., Park/Madison Aves., 212-752-8200, www.club macanudo.com; hours: M–Tu 12PM–1AM, W–Sa 12PM–1:30AM, Su 12PM–8PM)* is for those who like to smoke cigars while swilling a single malt. (Yes! You can still smoke here.) It's pricey and you need to dress up. **Bemelmans Bar (31)** *(Carlyle Hotel, 35 E. 76th St. at Madison Ave., 212-744-1600, www.thecarlyle.com; daily 12PM–11:30PM)* is classic New York—a gentleman's club ambience with plush chairs, cozy décor, steep drinks, and wonderful live jazz. If all this is a bit too mature for your taste, there's another, more youthful, aspect to the Upper East Side's bar and club scene, as represented by **Brother Jimmy's Bait Shack (32)** *(1644 Third Ave., at E. 92nd St., 212-426-2020, www.brotherjimmys.com;*

hours: M–Th 5PM–12AM, F 5PM–11AM, Sa 12PM–1AM, Su 12PM–11PM), a frat-boy paradise with beer and barbecues. Be warned. In a similar vein there's also **Iggy's (33)** *(1452 Second Ave., E. 75th/E. 76th Sts., 212-327-3043; hours: daily 12PM–4AM)*, where a lethal combo of cheap beers and even cheaper music can be had every night.

WHERE TO SHOP

The Upper East Side's prime shopping strip is Madison Avenue, where all the famous designers have their flagship stores. Parisian-style merchant **Hermès (34)** *(691 Madison Ave. at E. 62nd St., 212-751-3181, www.hermes.com; hours: M–W 10AM–6PM, Th 10AM–7PM, F–Sa 10AM–6PM)* offers its famous scarves and much more at this spacious store. If you're a foot fetishist, then **Jimmy Choo (35)** *(716 Madison Ave., E. 63rd/E. 64th Sts., 212-759-7078, www.jimmychoo.com; hours: Th 10AM–7PM, M–W, F–Sa 10AM–6PM, Su 12PM–6PM)* is your Nirvana. You can find sexy high-heeled creations that will make you feel part of the *Sex and the City* cast. **Barneys New York (36)** *(660 Madison Ave. at E. 61st St., 212-826-8900, www.barneys.com; hours: M–F 10AM–8PM, Sat 10AM–7PM, Su 11AM–6PM)* has classic menswear and women's

clothes too, as well as a beauty store, a super-cool restaurant, and price tags that read like fiction. **Prada (37)** *(841 Madison Ave. at E. 70th St., 212-327-4200, www.prada.com; hours: M–W 10AM–6PM, Th 10AM–7PM, F–Sa 10AM–6PM)* sells a whole range of men and women's wear, but it's those shoes with the little red tag on the heel that really count. **Morgane Le Fay (38)** *(980 Madison Ave., E. 76th/E. 77th Sts., 212-879-9700, www.morganelefay.com; hours: M–Sa 10AM–6PM, Su 12PM–5PM)* offers beautifully bizarre, almost architectural gowns and dresses at suitably architectural prices. Less expensive stores can be found east of Lexington Avenue. Ratcheting down the prices considerably is the **Memorial Sloan-**

Kettering Cancer Center Thrift Shop (39) *(1440 Third Ave., E. 81st/E. 82nd Sts., 212-535-1250; hours: M–F 10AM–5:30 PM, Sa 11AM–5PM)*, which has some real bargains, as the ladies who lunch often drop off their unwanted couture here. This is one of the best thrift shops in the city. At **Pookie & Sebastian (40)** *(1488 Second Ave., E. 77th/E. 78th Sts., 212-861-0550; hours: M–Sa 11AM–9PM, Su 11AM–7PM)* you can get cutting-edge fashion, including a whole array of designer jeans, at much reduced prices. Finally, if you're a hi-fi nut, **Lyric Hi-Fi, Inc. (41)** *(1221 Lexington Ave., E. 82nd/E. 83rd Sts., 212-439-1900, www.lyricusa.com; hours: M–Sa 10AM–6PM)* has great offers on a wide range of stuff and a knowledgeable staff.

WHERE TO STAY

If money's no object you can't beat the venerable **Carlyle Hotel (42)** *($$$$)* *(35 E. 76th St., Madison/Park Aves., 212-744-1600, www.thecarlyle.com)*. It has **Bemelmans Bar (31)** *(see "Bars & Nightlife," on page 181)*, famous for its animal murals by Ludwig Bemelmans, the creator of the *Madeleine* books, who was a former resident of the hotel. There's live music with a steep cover, but it's worth it. The 100-year-old **Hotel Wales (43)** *($$-$$$)* *(1295 Madison Ave. at E. 92nd St., 212-876-6000, www.waleshotel.com)* is a lovely hotel that feels like you're entering a private (albeit grand) house. It's also very pet- and child-friendly. There is also the **Gracie Inn (44)** *($$-$$$)* *(502 E. 81st. St., York/East End Aves., 212-628-1700, www.gracieinnhotel.com)*, tucked away in a town house far from the subway but well worth it.

CENTRAL PARK

To East Side of the Park:
4 5 to 59th St. or 86th St.; **6** to 59th St., 68th St.,
77th St., 86th St., 96th St., 103rd St., 110th St.

To West Side of the Park:
B C to 59th St.-Columbus Circle, 72nd St., 81st St.,
86th St., 96th St., 103rd St., 110th St.-Cathedral
Parkway; **A** to 59th St.-Columbus Circle

To Southern Side of the Park:
B D E to Seventh Ave.;
N Q R to 57th St.-Seventh Ave.;
F to 57th St.; **N R Q** to Fifth Ave.-59th St.

To Northern Side of the Park:
2 3 to Central Park North-110th St.

● SNAPSHOT ●

It's impossible to conceive of New York
without ★**CENTRAL PARK**, yet for years the
city existed without any major public park
for its teeming citizens. Old photographs

TOP PICK!

and engravings reveal a rocky expanse complete with

wooden shacks, grazing goats, swamps,
and encampments of the city's dispos-
sessed. In the mid-19th century, the
city's elders were finally piqued by
their great rivals in London and Paris
to do something about this, and

commissioned landscape designer Frederick Law Olmsted and architect Calvert Vaux to convert a vast chunk of this unruly land into a picturesque European-style park worthy of a great city. This of course they did (along with several other parks in New York), and the results were astonishing. Not only did New York gain an enormous and beautiful green space, but the effect was also to galvanize development around the park, turning what even in the 1880s was still a largely undeveloped rural suburb of the city into a social and architectural center every bit the equal of its European counterparts.

PLACES TO SEE
Landmarks:
Southern Section (Central Park South to 72nd Street):
Olmsted and Vaux adopted the three principal elements of 18th-century British Picturesque design—water, landscaping, and architecture—to create their master-piece, and these elements have only improved with time. Enter Central Park from the southeast and you'll encounter **The Pond (45)** *(approx. Fifth/Sixth Aves. between 60th/62nd Sts.)*—an artfully placed body of water with ducks and swans floating on it. Turn around and gaze south over The Pond at the skyline of Central

Park South rising above it for one of the most knockout views in the city. Just north of The Pond is the **Wollman Rink (46)** *(just north of the park entrance at Sixth Ave./Central Park South, www.wollmanskating rink.com: M–Tu 10AM–2:30PM,*

W–Th 10AM–10PM, *F–Sa* 10AM–11PM, *Su* 10AM–9PM)—a rival to the Rink at Rockefeller Center for the most romantic spot in the city. Built in the 1950s, it fell into disrepair, with the city unable to restore it. Enter Donald Trump on a white horse, who not only repaired it ahead of schedule, but did so $750,000 under budget. Naturally, it's now emblazoned with his name. Just north of the rink is **The Dairy (47)** *(mid-park at 65th St.)*, Vaux's delightful Victorian Gothic confection. It used to be a real working dairy, but now operates as an information center for the park, and its official gift store *(212-794-6564 for details)*. The other major landmarks in this southern section of the park are the **Central Park Zoo (48)** *(830 Fifth Ave., E. 63rd/E. 66th Sts., 212-439-6500, www.centralparkzoo.org; hours: Nov–March 10AM–4:30PM, April–Oct 10AM–5PM, weekends and holidays 10AM–5:30PM)* and the **Heckscher Playground (49)** *(Seventh Ave., W. 61st/W. 63rd Sts.)*. The biggest open space in the southern section of the park is the **Sheep Meadow (50)** *(starts at 66th St.)*, a designated quiet zone where sheep used to graze until as late as 1934. Nearby is **Strawberry Fields (51)** *(W. 72nd St at Central Park West)*, a former favorite spot of John Lennon, who lived in the Dakota Apartments across from the park. If you're a Beatles fan it may be a must; if not, be warned: it's often full of sappy guitar-twanging mourners paying "tribute."

Mid-Park (72nd through 79th Sts.):

North and slightly east is **The Lake (52)**, with its beautiful **Loeb Boathouse (53)** *(mid-park at 75th St.)* and charming **Bow Bridge (54)**. You can rent boats and even a gondola here. Near the lake is the lovely **Bethesda Fountain and Terrace (55)** *(mid-park, by the 72nd St. Transverse Rd.)*, which is one of the social hives of the park, full of every type of character on earth on a hot summer's day. **The Ramble (56)** *(mid-park from 72nd through 79th Sts.)*, where pathways twist amongst brush and trees, is east of the Lake, and one of the best places for bird watching. Just north of the Ramble are two architectural landmarks, the **Delacorte Theater (57)** *(mid-park at 80th St., see page 190)* and **Belvedere Castle (58)** *(mid-park at 79th St.)*—a Victorian stone block fantasy that rises majestically to the highest point in the park, offering superb views. It's also the location of the **Henry Luce Nature Observatory (58)** *(see page 189, hours: Tu–Su 10AM–5PM)*. As you move north over the 79th Street Transverse Road you come across a sweeping open expanse—**The Great Lawn (59)** *(mid-park, 79th/86th Sts.)*. A reservoir until the 1930s, it then became the place for New Yorkers to fool around—socializing, flirting, playing games, or just plain soaking up the sun. During the summer the Met and the Philharmonic stage free operas and concerts here, and the Lawn has played host to huge shows by the likes of Simon and Garfunkel and Garth Brooks. A reservoir still exists north of the 86th Street Transverse Road, now renamed **Jacqueline Kennedy Onassis Reservoir (60)** *(mid-park, 85th/96th Sts.)*. She was one of the thousands of people who used the popular jogging path around it, which is still in use.

North Section (97th through 110th Sts.):

North of the 97th Street Transverse Road at mid-park is the **North Meadow Recreation Center (61)**, a handsomely restored recreation facility set amidst the 23 acres of the North Meadow. The northernmost reaches of the park are some of the most beautiful and contrasting, with the wild beauty of the 11-acre **Harlem Meer (62)** *(NE corner of the park, 106th/109th Sts.),* a lake where you can fish from mid-April through mid-October, and the formal landscaping of the **Conservatory Garden (63)** *(Fifth Ave. at E. 105th St., 212-360-2766; hours: 8AM–dusk).*

Arts & Entertainment:

In Central Park it's hard to distinguish between kids' and adults' entertainment, so check out "Kids" on page 190 as well. For information on all activities, prices, and admission times, visit www.centralpark.org. If you're into fishing (strictly catch-and-release), the **Charles A. Dana Discovery Center (64)** *(Malcolm X Blvd. at 110th St., 212-860-1370)* will rent you equipment for fishing in nearby Harlem Meer. You can also meet up for bird-watching tours here, as well as take part in various family and children's workshops. Bird-watching and history tours also depart from the **Henry Luce Nature Observatory (58)**, which has microscopes, exhibits, and interactive displays for children, too. The **North Meadow Recreation Center (61)** *(mid-park at 97th St., 212-348-4867)* was converted from stables to a recreation center in the 1990s and offers soccer, softball, and 12 baseball fields for school and public use. Balls, bats, and other equipment can be rented inexpensively. For culture lovers, there are the **summer outdoor music shows** *(see www.summerstage.org or www.centralparknyc.org for details)*, with everything from classical concerts by the New York Philharmonic to free rock concerts. Every summer the **Delacorte Theater (57)** *(mid-park at 80th St., www.publictheater.org)* presents its free annual Shakespeare in the Park Festival, featuring big name talent (e.g., Jimmy Smits, Patrick Stewart). There's also a host of other activities you can do, from chess to biking to blading. (Equipment for all three can be rented in the park.)

Kids:

The **Heckscher Playground (49)** *(Seventh Ave., 61st/63rd Sts.)* is the biggest playground in Central Park (three acres), filled with swings and other amusements, plus excellent bathrooms. **The Carousel (65)** *(mid-park at 65th St.)* offers rides on beautiful hand-painted wooden horses for two dollars; it's an attraction that's been going since 1871. The **Wollman Rink (46)** *(just north of the park entrance at Sixth Ave./59th St., www.wollmanskating rink.com, 212-439-6900)* is a year-round attraction for children and adults alike. In the winter you can arrange

for children's special skating classes with qualified teachers, and in the summer the rink is transformed into a delightful family center with a mini-carousel, rides, face-painting, games, cotton candy, and all kinds of other attractions.

chapter 8

HARLEM & SPANISH HARLEM
MORNINGSIDE HEIGHTS
WASHINGTON HEIGHTS & INWOOD

The **Central Park Zoo (48)** *(830 Fifth Ave., 63rd/66th Sts., 212-439-6500, www.centralparkzoo.org)*, of course, is the biggest children's attraction, and there are actually two of them—the **Tisch Children's Zoo (66)**, which is essentially a petting zoo with goats, sheep, and other domestic animals, and the main zoo itself, home to polar bears, sea lions, penguins, and much more, all painstakingly arranged in simulations of their natural habitats. If you can afford it, there are even overnight pajama parties for kids to learn about the animals. Avoid the lackluster food at the café.

PLACES TO EAT & DRINK
Where to Eat:

There are the classic hot dog and pretzel stands dotted around the park, or you can try the **Central Park Boathouse Restaurant (67) ($$)** *(see Loeb Boathouse on page 187) (mid-park at 75th St., 212-517-2233; hours: Apr–Nov M–F 12PM–4PM and 5:30PM–9:30PM, Sa–Su 9:30AM–4PM and 6PM–9:30PM; Nov–Apr M–F 12PM–4PM, Sa–Su 9:30AM–4PM)*, though it can be expensive and pretty limited.

HARLEM & SPANISH HARLEM MORNINGSIDE HEIGHTS WASHINGTON HEIGHTS & INWOOD

Places to See:
1. Apollo Theater
2. Strivers' Row
3. Hamilton Heights Historic District
4. Abyssinian Baptist Church
5. Mount Morris Park
6. Trinity Cemetery
7. Graffiti Hall of Fame
8. Schomburg Center for Research in Black Culture
9. Studio Museum in Harlem
10. National Black Theater
11. Museo del Barrio
12. Museum of the City of New York
30. Cathedral Church of St. John the Divine
31. Columbia University
32. Low Memorial Library
33. Morningside Park
34. Riverside Church
35. Grant's Tomb
45. George Washington Bridge
46. Fort Tryon Park
47. Cloisters Museum
48. Inwood Hill Park
49. Henry Hudson Bridge
50. Morris-Jumel Mansion

Places to Eat & Drink:
13. Amy Ruth's
14. Londel's Supper Club
15. Dinosaur Bar-B-Que
16. Uptown Juice Bar
17. Sylvia's
18. Piatto d'Oro
19. Cotton Club
20. Lenox Lounge
21. Showman's Bar
22. St. Nick's Pub
36. Kitchenette Uptown
37. Max Soha
38. Terrace in the Sky
39. Bistro Ten 18
40. Hungarian Pastry Shop
41. Le Monde
42. Heights Bar and Grill
51. New Leaf Café
52. Kismat Indian Restaurant
53. 107 West

Sometimes I feel discriminated against,
but it does not make me angry.
It merely astonishes me.
How can anyone deny themselves
the pleasure of my company?

—Zora Neale Hurston

HARLEM & SPANISH HARLEM

HARLEM: **B** **C** *to 110th St.-Cathedral Parkway,*
116th St., 125th St., 135th St., 145th St.;
B **D** *to 155th St.;* **2** **3** *to Central Park North-*
110th St., 116th St., 125th St., 135th St.;
3 *to 145 St.;* **4** **5** **6** *to 125 St.*

SPANISH HARLEM: **6** *to 96th St., 103rd St.,*
110th St., 116th St., 125 St.; **4** **5** *to 125th St.*

● SNAPSHOT ●

Visitors to Manhattan often stop short north of Central
Park, or at the most take a trip to the Cloisters Museum
at Manhattan's far northern tip, which is a shame,
because the numerous and varied neighborhoods of this
area are fascinating places to explore. Harlem *(110th St.
to the Harlem River, Morningside/Saint Nicholas Aves.),*
the most famous, has been a center of African-American
life in New York since the early years of the 20th century, and after a long period of turbulence in the 1960s
and 1970s, is undergoing a major renaissance, with its
historic buildings being restored by homesteaders
(both black and white) and new capital
injected into its stores and businesses.
Spanish Harlem *(E. 96th St. to E.
120th Sts., approx., Fifth/Third
Aves.),* or El Barrio ("The
Neighborhood"), as it's called
by its largely Puerto Rican

population, has yet to attract the influx of capital that Harlem has, but is still well worth visiting for its street life and delicious, inexpensive food.

PLACES TO SEE
Landmarks:

One of the most famous landmarks is the **Apollo Theater (1)** *(253 W. 125th St., Adam Clayton Powell Jr. Blvd./Frederick Douglass Blvd., 212-531-5305, www.apollotheater.com).* It was here that Michael Jackson, Ella Fitzgerald, and a host of other R&B and soul stars got their start. The TV program *Showtime at the Apollo* is broadcast from here every week; it's a funny and enjoyable musical contest to watch, but is brutal for contestants the audience doesn't like. The venue also hosts major rock stars such as Van Morrison when they're looking for smaller places with old-time ambience. Harlem has some of the best 19th-century residential architecture in the country, now in a flurry of restoration in many places. Check out **Strivers' Row (2)** *(W. 138th to W. 139th Sts., Powell/Douglass Blvds.),* a block of beautiful Renaissance-style brick row houses, designed in part by McKim, Mead & White in 1890. As the area became increasingly African-American, the black middle classes moved into the block and the term "Strivers' Row" gained popular usage. The other major area for handsome row houses is in the **Hamilton Heights Historic District (3)** *(W. 140th/W. 145th Sts., Amsterdam/Edgecomb Aves.).*

In particular, note the lovely houses on Convent Avenue, near W. 148th Street, with their curving stoops and bay windows. The **Abyssinian Baptist Church (4)** *(132 Odell Clark Pl., formerly West 138th St., Adam Clayton Powell, Jr./Malcolm X Blvds., also known as 7th and Lenox Aves., 212-862-7474, www.abyssinian.org)* is the most well-known of Harlem's numerous churches and offers wonderful services with gospel singing. If you're interested in gospel tours of Harlem, many companies offer them, generally with brunch or drinks included. (Note that large groups are required to register with this and other churches in advance, especially on Sundays.) Harlem has several lovely parks and open spaces, and **Mount Morris Park (5)** *(W. 120th/W. 124th Sts., Madison Ave./Mount Morris Park West)*, also known as Marcus Garvey Park, is the most historic. Only a few years ago many of the houses surrounding it were simply shells, or grimly hanging on as rooming houses, but the establishment of a Historic District and the recent frenzy of restoration, by whites, African-Americans, and Caribbeans alike, has restored these buildings to their original splendor. **Trinity Cemetery (6)** *(W. 153rd/W. 155th Sts., Riverside Dr./ Amsterdam Ave.)* has some of the oldest graves in the city (including those of notable New Yorkers John James Audubon and John Jacob Astor), with great views over the Hudson River. In Spanish Harlem, check out the **Graffiti Hall of Fame (7)** *(W. 106th St., Madison/Park Aves.)*, where the long walls are covered in brilliantly colored images by masters, old-school and otherwise.

Arts & Entertainment:

As befits a neighborhood so rich in cultural history—with figures such as writers Zora Neale Hurston and Langston Hughes, and musicians Fats Waller, Duke Ellington, and Louis Armstrong; all lived or worked there in the 1920s and 1930s—Harlem has a large number of first-class cultural institutions. Its musical heritage is kept alive in its clubs and bars *(see "Bars & Nightlife," page 200)*, but for a general cultural record of black America the **Schomburg Center for Research in Black Culture (8)** *(515 Malcolm X Blvd. at W. 135th St., 212-491-2200, www.nypl.org/locations/schomburg; hours: M–W 12PM–8PM, Th–F 11AM–6PM, Sa 10AM–5PM)* can't be beat. The center offers a permanent collection of documents, books, films, and more, and excellent exhibitions—a genuinely moving and informative experience that can be appreciated by all, no matter what your ethnicity. The **Studio Museum in Harlem (9)** *(144 W. 125th St., Malcolm X/Adam Clayton Powell Jr. Blvds., 212-864-4500, www.studiomuseum.org, cash only; hours: W–F 12PM–6PM, Sa 10AM–6PM, Su 12PM–6PM)* was founded in 1968 as a space in which to exhibit work by black artists, both American and foreign. It offers such programming as lecture series, artists in residence, and extremely varied exhibitions from painters and sculptors to African comic artists. The **National Black Theater (10)** *(2031 Fifth Ave., W. 125th/W. 126th Sts., 212-722-3800, www.nationalblacktheatre.org)* is an enormous 64,000 square-foot building that's broken up inside into a number of much smaller, more intimate performing areas, decorated with African art and décor. Plays and other forms of performances here emphasize black culture and history. Spanish Harlem has its own equivalent to the Studio Museum in Harlem, the **Museo del Barrio (11)** *(1230 Fifth Ave., E. 104th/E. 105th Sts., 212-831-7272, www.elmuseo.org; hours: W–Su 11AM–6PM)*. It has a large and varied collection of works by Latino artists, both living abroad and resident in the U.S., as well as excellent temporary exhibits. The **Museum of the City of New York (12)** *(1220 Fifth Ave., E. 103rd/E. 104th Sts., 212-534-1672, www.mcny.org; hours: Tu–Su 10AM–5PM)* houses a delightful collection of artifacts that reveal the history of the city from colonial times to the present, including photographs, paintings, and documents. There's also a touching collection of more personal effects such as children's toys, diaries, and other ephemera.

PLACES TO EAT & DRINK
Where to Eat:

Don't come to Harlem expecting to eat light: soul food is the name of the game here, and it's the best in the city. At **Amy Ruth's (13) ($)** *(113 W. 116th St., Lenox/Seventh Aves., 212-280-8779, www.amyruthsharlem.com; hours: M 11:30AM–11PM, Tu–Th 8:30AM–11PM, F 8:30AM–5:30AM, Sa 7:30AM–5:30AM, Su 7:30AM–11PM)* you'll get stuffed for a very reasonable cost in an extremely friendly atmosphere. **Londel's Supper Club (14) ($$)** *(2620 Frederick Douglass Blvd., W. 139th/W. 140th Sts., 212-234-6114, www.londelsrestaurant.com; hours: Tu–Sa 11:30AM–12AM, Su 11AM–5PM)* does a sterling Sunday brunch and has some of the best soul food in town.

If you're in the mood for barbeque, head to **Dinosaur Bar-B-Que (15) ($)** *(646 W. 131st St., Riverside Dr./Broadway, 212-694-1777, www.dinosaurbarbque.com; hours: M–Th 11:30AM–11PM, F–Sa 11:30AM–12AM, Su 12PM–10PM)* for your fill of fried green tomatoes, creole spiced deviled eggs, and lots of other tasty, finger-lickin' grub. Get your okra, collards and mac'n'cheese at the vegetarian Caribbean spot **Uptown Juice Bar (16) ($)** *(54 W. 125th St., Lenox/5th Aves., 212-987-2660; hours: daily 8AM–10PM)*. They make a mean honey-barbequed tofu—who said you can't have veggie bbq with some soul? **Sylvia's (17) ($)** *(328 Lenox Ave., 126th/127th Sts., 212-996-0660, www.sylviassoulfood.com; hours: M–Sa 8AM–10:30PM, Su 11AM–8PM)* opened in 1962 with a seating capacity of 35. It now seats up to 450 and is a world-famous historic restaurant serving up soul food classics. At **Piatto d'Oro (18) ($$)** *(349 E. 109th St. at First Ave., 212-828-2929, www.restaurantpiattodoro.com; hours: daily 11AM–10PM)* you'll find inventive and delicious risottos and fish dishes in large portions.

Bars & Nightlife:

Harlem is hopping with nightlife, and historic jazz venues. Call ahead or visit the clubs' web sites for specific show times. The tiny **Cotton Club (19)** *(656 W. 125th St. at Riverside Dr., 212-663-7890, www.cottonclub-newyork. com)* has a great band and offers dining and cocktails as well as brunch specials. (This isn't the 1923 Cotton Club, but a newer venture established in 1978.) The **Lenox Lounge (20)** *(288 Malcolm X Blvd., W. 124th/W. 125th Sts., 212-427-0253, www.lenoxlounge.com)*, however, is still in its original location, and its Deco décor and live jazz can waft you back on a serious time trip. **Showman's Bar (21)** *(375 W. 125th St., St. Nicholas/Morningside Aves., 212-864-8941),* established in 1942, is one of Harlem's genuine jazz treasures; drinks are inexpensive and it's all about the music here. **St. Nick's Pub (22)** *(773 St. Nicholas Ave. at W. 149th St., 212-283-9728, www.stnicksjazz pub.net; hours: M–Th 1PM–3AM, F–Sa 4PM–4AM)* is a crammed-full space that offers live jazz for a very reasonable cover (plus free soul food), seven days a week.

WHERE TO SHOP

Money has come to Harlem in a big way recently, and although this has had a very obvious beneficial effect, it's also burdened Harlem with some of the more soulless commercial glitz of downtown, such as the vast Harlem USA Complex (23) *(300 W. 125th St., Adam Clayton Powell Jr./Frederick Douglass Blvds.),* though if you want the latest sneakers or street wear it comes in handy. For more personal stores check out the open-air Malcolm Shabazz Harlem Market (24) *(52 W. 116th St. at Malcolm X Blvd., 212-987-8131; hours: daily 10AM–8PM),* which sells wonderful African fabrics, clothes, and crafts. With its mission to "inspire, motivate, and educate," the Hue-Man Bookstore & Café (25) *(2319 Frederick Douglass Blvd., 124th/125th Sts., 212-665-7400, www.huemanbookstore. com; hours: M–Sa 10AM–8PM, Su 11AM–7PM)* is one of the largest, independent African-American bookstores in the country. They have frequent book signings by celebrity authors, discussions, performances, and children's story hours. If all your book-browsing leaves you a little hungry, satisfy your sweet tooth with a cupcake from Tonnie's Minis (26) *(264 Lenox Ave., 123rd/124th Sts., 212-881-5292, www.tonniesminis.com; hours: M–F 7:30AM–9PM, Sa 9AM–9PM, Su 10AM–7PM)*. You can get your individual cupcake made-to-order with whatever cake and frosting pairing you choose. Tonnie's signature cupcake is the "Carrot Dream"—he's the only one that prepares it to ensure that the recipe remains a secret! Top it off with ice cream if it's a hot day. In Spanish Harlem, the main shopping strip is along East 116th Street (27), which has become increasingly Mexican of late. There are plenty of small food vendors and stores known as botanicas, that sell candles and religious charms and icons. They're well worth visiting because botanicas are disappearing at a fast rate in the city as real estate developments roll over them.

WHERE TO STAY

Harlem has a number of bed-and-breakfast inns, which are an intimate and easy way to get a feel for the neighborhood. The Sugar Hill Harlem Inn (28) *($$-$$$)* *(460 W. 141st St., Amsterdam/Convent Aves., 212-234-5432, www.sugarhillharleminn.com)* features rooms that are named after great artists associated with the area, such as "Ella's Room" and "Miles Room." The 1906 Victorian town house has been beautifully restored to preserve the historical details of the building. The Harlem Flophouse (29) *($)* *(242 W. 123rd St., 212-662-0678, www.harlemflophouse.com)* is even more reasonably priced in another handsomely restored old building. There's a communal dining room and garden.

MORNINGSIDE HEIGHTS

Ⓑ Ⓒ *to Cathedral Parkway-110th St., 116th St.,*
125th St.; ❶ *to Cathedral Parkway-110th St.,*
116th St.-Columbia University, 125th St.

● **SNAPSHOT** ●

Morningside Heights is "college town," thanks to its vast student and faculty population, including Columbia University and Barnard College, among many others. This makes it an ideal place to stroll while checking out the wonderful campus buildings and the inexpensive bars, cafes, and restaurants that cluster around them. The main shopping and eating drag is Broadway from 110th to 116th streets, though there are many places tucked away in the side streets. Recently, the term "SoHa"—"South of Harlem"—has been applied to the neighborhood by real estate agents, an odious term but one that marks the notable trend for Upper West Siders to shift ever north-wards in search of reasonably priced accommodation.

PLACES TO SEE
Landmarks:

The great landmark here—one of New York's finest—is the truly astonishing **Cathedral Church of St. John the Divine (30)** *(1047 Amsterdam Ave. at 112th St., 212-316-7540, www.stjohndivine.org)*. St. John's size has to be seen to be believed; it's bigger than Notre Dame and Chartres cathedrals in France combined, and the Statue of Liberty would fit beneath her dome. Her famous

Rose Window is the largest stained glass window in the country. St. John's was begun in 1892 and is still far from finished, as the empty niches on the exterior make clear. Teams of sculptors are still working on her today, and as a result the church represents a number of architectural styles. Tours of the grounds and interior are available. If you're here in October, don't miss the annual Blessing of the Animals as part of the Feast of St. Francis, when animals from horses and snakes to gerbils and rats parade up the aisle with their owners. The other major institution here is **Columbia University (31)** *(main entrance: Broadway at W. 116th St., 212-854-4900, www.columbia.edu)*, designed by Charles McKim of the famous architectural firm McKim, Mead & White in grand Beaux Arts style. The centerpiece is the **Low Memorial Library (32)**, a classical porticoed temple around which the other campus buildings are clustered. The campus is open to the public, though you need to be part of the regular student-led tours to visit the interior elements. Visitors should head to the Visitors Center in the Low Library for information. **Morningside Park (33)** *(W. 110th/W. 123rd Sts., Morningside Ave./ Morningside Dr., www.morningsidepark.org)* is a narrow band of parkway that separates Harlem from Morningside Heights. You really get a sense of the dramatic, rocky nature of Manhattan's topography here, before so much was flattened out for development. The views of St. John's are amazing. **Riverside Church (34)** *(490 Riverside Dr. at W. 120th St., 212-870-6700, www.theriversidechurchny.org; hours: daily 7AM–10PM)* is one of the city's great landmarks, a Rockefeller-funded project that rises 21 stories and has a not-to-be-missed observation deck in its bell tower. **Grant's Tomb (35)** *(Riverside Dr. at W. 122nd St., www.nps.gov/gegr; hours: daily 9AM–5PM),* formerly known as the General Grant National Memorial, was the city's number one tourist attraction in the early years of the 20th century. Its attraction has waned, but this domed classical monument is still worth a visit and is open daily.

PLACES TO EAT & DRINK
Where to Eat:
Kitchenette Uptown (36) ($) *(1272 Amsterdam Ave., W. 122nd/W. 123rd Sts., 212-531-7600, www.kitchenette restaurant.com; hours: M–F 8AM–11PM, Sa–Su 9AM–11PM)* is a tiny spot and a favorite with college students and others on a tight budget who want succulent soul food and other southern-fried delights. Next door there's **Max Soha (37) ($$)** *(1274 Amsterdam Ave. at W. 123rd St., 212-531-2221, www.maxsoha.com, cash only; hours: daily 12PM–12AM),* serving can't-go-wrong Italian food at great prices, though its popularity means the lines can be long. If you don't mind shelling out some serious cash, **Terrace in the Sky (38) ($$$)** *(400 W. 119th St., Amsterdam Ave./Morningside Dr., 212-666-9490, www.terraceinthe sky.com; hours: lunch F 12PM–2:30PM, dinner Tu–Sa 5:30PM–10:30PM, brunch Su 11AM–3PM)* offers stunning views from its penthouse location. It serves terrific Mediterranean and French cuisine. On 110th Street there's the excellent **Bistro Ten 18 (39) ($$)** *(1018 Amsterdam Ave. at W. 110th St., 212-662-7600, www. bistroten18.com: M–F 12PM–3PM and 5PM–11PM, Sa 11AM–3PM and 5PM–11PM, Su 11AM–3PM and 5PM–*

10PM) for simple well-produced American fare with a great view of the Cathedral Church of St. John the Divine (30). The **Hungarian Pastry Shop (40) ($)** *(1030 Amsterdam Ave., W. 110th/W. 111th Sts., 212-866-4230; hours: M–F 7:30AM–11:30PM, Sa 8:30AM–11:30PM, Su 8:30AM–10:30PM)* is an Eastern European classic in the heart of college town. You can't beat its *sacher tortes* and *linzer tarts*, washed down with strong Viennese coffee.

Bars & Nightlife:

An amble down Broadway between about W. 110th and W. 116th streets reveals a large number of bars and cafes, all frequented by Columbia students and faculty. **Le Monde (41)** *(2885 Broadway, W. 112th/W. 113th Sts., 212-531-3939, www.lemondenyc.com; hours: M–Th 9:30AM–12AM, F–Sa 9:30AM–1AM, Su 9:30AM–12AM)* is a brasserie with good beer and atmosphere. The **Heights Bar and Grill (42)** *(2867 Broadway, W. 111th/W. 112th Sts., 212-866-7035, www.theheightsnyc.com; hours: bar open daily until 3AM)* has a (teensy) rooftop bar and offers cheap Mexican food washed down with margaritas.

WHERE TO SHOP

Mondel Chocolates (43) *(2913 Broadway at W. 114th St., 212-864-2111, www.mondelchocolates.com; hours: M–Sa 11AM–7PM, Su 12PM–6PM)* has been going since 1943, and its old-fashioned vibe is the secret to its success. The Bank Street Bookstore (44) *(610 W. 112th St. at Broadway, 212-678-1654, www.bankstreetbooks.com; M–W 11AM–7PM, Th 10AM–8PM, F–Sa 10AM–6PM, Su 11AM–6PM)* is an excellent children's bookstore with a highly knowledgeable staff.

WASHINGTON HEIGHTS & INWOOD

WASHINGTON HEIGHTS: C to 155th St., 163rd St.-Amsterdam Ave., 168th St.-Washington Heights; **A** to 168th St.-Washington Heights, 175th St., 181st St., 190th St., Dyckman St.; **1** to 157th St., 168th St., 181st St., 191st St., Dyckman St.

INWOOD: A to Inwood-207th St.; **1** to 207th St., 215th St.

● SNAPSHOT ●

Most New Yorkers live their entire lives never knowing what lies at Manhattan's northern tip. The answer is some of the best parks in the city, one of its best museums, great street life, and views of the Hudson River and of the New Jersey Palisades that can't be beat. It's definitely worth the trip. Washington Heights *(W. 155th/Dyckman, a.k.a. 200th, Sts., between the Hudson and Harlem Rivers)* and Inwood *(north of Dyckman St. between the Hudson and Harlem Rivers)* both used to be the sites of large estates and remained among the last parts of New York to be urbanized until the subway systems reached them in the 1930s. Washington Heights is home to one of the largest Dominican populations in the city, but its parks and handsome apartment buildings have also become attractive recently to non-Hispanics, especially young artists, forced northwards by ever-escalating real estate prices. At its northern end is Fort Tryon Park, laid out by Frederick Law Olmsted (son of the Olmsted of Central Park fame) and home to the stunning Cloisters Museum, where the Metropolitan Museum maintains its medieval collection. Inwood has a relatively small residential population and a beautiful park, Inwood Hill Park, where some of the last primeval forest in Manhattan can be found.

PLACES TO SEE
Landmarks:

The **George Washington Bridge (45)** *(spanning the Hudson River at 179th St.),* one of New York's most amazing pieces of engineering (and lit up beautifully at night), can best be viewed from Fort Washington Avenue, which runs parallel to the waterfront. The virgin peaks on the far side, known as the Palisades, which are at their best in the fall, were bought up by the Rockefeller family to prevent development, perhaps the greatest of their many philanthropic acts. Washington Avenue eventually leads to **Fort Tryon Park (46)** *(W. 190th St. to Riverside Dr.),* a park that combines careful landscaping with the wild and rocky natural topography of the site. In the summer it's a favorite spot for weddings, and the views of both the city to the east and the Palisades across the river are breathtaking. The park is home to the **Cloisters Museum (47)** *(see page 209),* a branch of The

Metropolitan Museum of Art. **Inwood Hill Park (48)** *(north and west of Dyckman St. to the tip of Manhattan)* is the supposed site of original Dutch governor Peter Minuit's "purchase" of Manhattan from the Native American Lenapes in 1626, or so a plaque here will inform you. The park is densely filled in places with the last vestiges of the forest that once covered Manhattan from tip to tip. At the very northern end is the **Henry Hudson Bridge (49)**, and painted on the rocks nearby is the vast blue "C," for Columbia University, whose students play soccer and football at nearby Baker Field.

Arts & Entertainment:

The **Cloisters Museum (47)** *(Fort Washington Ave. at Margaret Corbin Plaza, 212-923-3700, www.met museum.org; hours: March–Oct Tu–Su 9:30AM–5:15PM; Nov–Feb Tu-Su 9:30AM–4:45PM)* is a miracle of money and vision. In the 1930s the Rockefeller family, which owned the land that's now Fort Tryon Park, purchased, shipped back home, and reassembled elements of five medieval cloisters from Europe. The Met now houses its medieval art collection here, but the real attraction is this exquisite architectural sanctuary, perhaps the most peaceful spot in all of New York City. Another lovely museum in this neighborhood is the **Morris-Jumel Mansion (50)** *(65 Jumel Terrace, W. 160th/W. 162nd Sts., 212-923-8008; hours: W–Su 10AM–4PM, M–Tu by appointment only)*, the oldest house in Manhattan and home to George Washington during parts of the Revolutionary War. It offers excellent tours of the house and grounds, as well as a number of children's programs.

PLACES TO EAT & DRINK
Where to Eat:

If you're visiting The Cloisters, the **New Leaf Café (51)** *(1 Margaret Corbin Dr. near Park Dr., 212-568-5323, www.newleafrestaurant.com; hours: Tu–F 12PM–3:30PM, Tu–Sa 6PM–10PM, Su 5:30PM–9:30PM, brunch Sa–Su 11AM–3:30PM)* is a great place to stop for a bite. The restaurant's views—there's a pleasant open-air terrace to enjoy in good weather—bring people back. Profits go toward Fort Tryon Park. Need curry in a hurry? In the Washington Heights area, you can pop into the popular **Kismat Indian Restaurant (52) ($)** *(603 Fort Washington Ave., at 187th St., 212-795-8633; hours: daily 12PM–11PM)*, a neighborhood institution. The menu is a mix of American, Southwest, and Cajun at **107 West (53) ($-$$)** *(811 W. 187th St., 212-923-3311, www.107west.com; call for hours)*. The fried chicken has fans.

Bars & Nightlife:

Washington Heights has always had a buzzing street life at night, but with gentrification has come a hip bar scene. **No Parking (54)** *(4168 Broadway, W. 176th/W. 177th Sts., 212-923-8700; www.noparkingbar.com; hours: Tu–Th 6PM–3AM, F 6PM–4AM, Sa 7PM–4AM, Su 7PM–3PM)* is a sleek lounge that caters to the gay crowd. The **Monkey Room Bar (55)** *(589 Fort Washington Ave. at*

W. 187th St., 212-543-9888, www.monkeyroomnyc.com; hours: daily 7AM–4AM) is a hip, eclectic spot that serves as a morning coffee shop as well as a DJ-heavy nightclub.

WHERE TO SHOP

It probably won't be the kind of couture you can pick up in the fancier nabes downtown, but at the Washington Heights branch of thrift store chain Goodwill Industries (56) *(512 W. 181st St. at Amsterdam Ave., 212-923-7910, www.goodwillny.org)* you might find a genuine Guayaberas shirt that'll look cool in the local bars. The Met has one of the best gift shops of all museums, and its branch at the Cloisters, Cloisters Gift Shop (57) *(see Cloisters Museum on page 209)* has plenty of fun medieval kitsch to take home as a memento. Or pick up a tasty memento at Carrot Top Pastries (58) *(3931 Broadway, 164th/165th Sts., 212-927-4800: M–Sa 6AM–9PM, Su 7AM–6PM)*, which arguably bakes up the best carrot cake in town, as well as other delicious delectables. Fashion, music, and art merge to create the high-end street wear available at Probus (59) *(714 W. 181st St. Bennett Ave./Broadway, 212-923-9153, www.probusnyc.com; hours: 10:30AM–8:30PM)*. Designer footwear, jeans, sunglasses, and more will have you looking smooth and stylish. If you're looking for authentic latin tunes, *baile* (dance) your way over to Quisqueya (60) *(52 Sherman Ave., Arden/Thayer Sts., 212-942-1020; hours: M–Sa 10AM–8PM)*. From salsa to meringue, and bachata to bolero, they stock over 25,000 CDs and records, including rare out-of-print albums. *Viva musica!*

INDEX

Yankee Stadium: 4 Train
51st St. — 161 St.

South St. Seaport, Pier
17, Yankees clubhouse shop,
Brooklyn Bridge: AC Train
51st St. — Fulton St.

Seinfeld Diner: E train
51st St. — 7 Ave. B
Train — Cathedral Pkwy

The Dakota: On the way
to Seinfeld Diner 72 St.

Guggenheim: 456 Train
51st St. — 86th St.

NOTES

WTC: E Train 51st St. —
World Trade Center

421 Broome St. (Heath Ledger):
6 Train: 51st St. — Spring St.

Bank of America Tower:
6 Train 51st St. — Grand Central
42nd St., 7 Train to 42nd
St. Bryant Park

Museum of Sex: 6 Train 51st
St. — 28th St.

Met Museum: 6 Train 51st St. —
77 St.

Times Square: 6 Train 51st
— Grand Central 42 St, 7 Train
— Times Square 42 St

Statue of Liberty: 5 Train
51st St. — Bowling Green

MLB Fan Cave: 6 Train
Astor Pl

Chinatown: 6 Train
Canal St

LaGuardia — 7 tram: Times
Square to 111 St.

NOTES

NOTES